KNIVES
MILITARY EDGED TOOLS & WEAPONS

Brassey's Modern Military Equipment
Series Editor: James Marchington

Current Titles:

Tanks: Main Battle and Light Tanks
Marsh Gelbart

Anti-Tank Weapons
John Norris

Handguns and Sub-Machine Guns
James Marchington

Knives: Military Edged Tools & Weapons
James Marchington

Forthcoming Titles:

NBC: Nuclear, Biological and Chemical Warfare
Will Fowler and John Norris

Assault Rifles, Rifles, Combat Shotguns
John Norris

Brassey's *Modern Military Equipment*

KNIVES
MILITARY EDGED TOOLS & WEAPONS

James Marchington

Copyright © 1997 Brassey's (UK) Ltd

First English Edition 1997

UK editorial offices: Brassey's, 33 John Street, London WC1N 2AT
UK orders: Marston Book Services, PO Box 269, Abingdon, OX14 4SD

North American orders: Brassey's Inc., PO Box 960,
Herndon, VA 22070, USA

James Marchington has asserted his moral right to be identified
as the author of this work.

Library of Congress Cataloging in Publication Data available

British Library Cataloguing in Publication Data
A catalogue record for this book is available from the British Library

ISBN 1 85753 163 9 Hardcover

Typeset & Designed by Harold Martin & Redman Ltd
Printed in Great Britain by The Amadeus Press Ltd, Huddersfield, West Yorkshire.

CONTENTS

v

Anyone who spends a significant part of his life outdoors soon comes to appreciate the value of a good knife. One of man's most basic tools, a knife is as versatile as the hand that holds it. It can gather and prepare food, build and tend a fire, cook, create a shelter, build a raft, signal for rescue, and much more. For the soldier, the knife is also a weapon - not often the weapon of choice, as its use demands that he is uncomfortably close to his enemy, but a weapon none the less, and one that can be both intimidating and lethally effective at close quarters.

A well-made knife offers something more to its owner - it is aesthetically pleasing and satisfying to use. People whose only use for a knife is to prepare the vegetables find this difficult to understand and readily confuse it with blood lust. In fact it is nothing of the sort. It is more akin to a craftsman's appreciation of a well-made tool, or a writer's preference for a fine fountain pen over a cheap ballpoint. The cheap and clumsy item may get the job done, but a quality instrument turns a chore into a pleasure.

For the outdoorsman or soldier, a knife is not a luxury; it is a necessity. The problem is knowing which knife to carry. For many camp and field chores a relatively small, single-edged blade may be the most convenient and practical. But if the situation turns out badly and your outing becomes a battle for survival, you may wish you had taken a heavier duty tool, capable of felling small trees and chopping logs. And if a soldier finds himself in hand-to-hand combat, a good field knife may be pitifully inadequate against a big fighting blade.

It is not often practicable to carry a selection of knives for specific uses - certainly not when you are travelling on foot. You have to choose a knife which offers a sensible compromise - one that is sufficiently light and convenient to carry, but hefty enough to tackle heavier jobs if necessary.

This is the thinking behind the many 'combat' knives produced today. A combat knife is designed to be a multi-purpose tool, capable of doing a reasonable job of the 1001 tasks that may be required of it by a soldier living and working in the field. Once or twice during his service this may include attacking an enemy, but meanwhile the

Special forces training: note the knife worn in an inverted sheath sewn onto the soldier's assault vest, where it is quickly accessible in an emergency to cut a tangled rope.

knife will be used daily for ordinary domestic chores.

This point is completely missed by those who demand that combat and survival knives should be banned - an attitude that has been prevalent in the British media during the time I was writing this book. The word 'combat' suggests to the ignorant that these knives are designed for the single purpose of killing. In fact they are designed to be truly multi-purpose, and are quite different in design from the pure fighting knives covered in the first chapter.

It is in any case dangerously naive to think that banning a particular class of inanimate object will change the behaviour of social misfits and violent criminals. However, this is not the place to debate that particular subject. This book is written not for the ignorant but for those who understand and appreciate the value of a good knife, both as a working tool and as an example of skilled design and craftsmanship.

I should perhaps explain the way I have categorised the knives described here. Of necessity, the book is divided **1** into sections for 'Fighting Knives', 'Bayonets', 'Combat and Survival Knives' and so on. In reality, knives do not lend themselves to such sweeping generalisation. Knife designs form a continuum, with no clear distinctions between one type and another. And besides, if a knife is what it does, then the definition is placed on it by the user, not the maker. If you find yourself having to survive in a hostile environment, then whatever knife you happen to have with you becomes your survival knife. Likewise, faced with an enemy determined to kill you, whatever blade comes to hand is pressed into service as a fighting weapon.

Every knife in this book is capable of being used for many different jobs, and probably has been at some time and place. The categories are mine and are based on my own interpretation of the circumstances in which I would choose to carry the individual knives. Their designers and makers, never mind other users, may well have different opinions.

The choice of which knives to feature is entirely personal too. I have tried to cover a full range of Western types, but it would be impossible in a book of this size to show every example and variation available throughout the world. I have barely touched on the thriving custom knife industry and have all but ignored the ethnic knives of non-Western cultures, many of which have deep religious significance as well as being practical tools. Such are the limitations of a book of this type: if I have omitted your personal favourites, I can only apologise.

Finally, I should like to thank all those people who have assisted me. Makers, wholesalers, retailers, collectors and enthusiasts have all freely given help and advice, and this book would not have been possible without them. In particular, Will Fowler's unstinting support and enthusiasm has been invaluable throughout the project. To him and all the others, too numerous to mention, thank you.

James Marchington
December 1996

FIGHTING KNIVES AND DAGGERS

A development of the famous Second World War Fairbairn-Sykes Commando Knife, the Applegate Fairbairn Fighting Knife was designed by Colonel Rex Applegate (of the US OSS) and Captain WE Fairbairn (of the British Royal Marines, and who had co-designed the F-S Dagger).

The A-F is a significant improvement on the F-S, which, despite its fame, had a number of shortcomings: it lacked strength at the tip and the tang, and the grip shape did not lend itself to alternative holds.

The A-F knife has a broader, stronger blade than the F-S, and the more rounded spear point gives much better strength at the tip. Also, the tang is considerably wider and stronger than that of the F-S. The blade is made of stainless steel, a considerable improvement on the basic carbon steel used in the wartime dagger.

The handle, too, has been improved beyond all recognition. Made of Lexan plastic, it is oval in cross-section and fills the hand well. The recess near the guard provides good control and aids withdrawal. The double guard is angled away from the hand, allowing alternative holds and minimising the chance of the guard's catching in clothing and the like.

The knife also has adjustable lead weights in the handle, so that one may alter the knife's balance to suit the particular style and preference.

All in all, this is a highly sophisticated fighting knife and a worthy successor to the famous F-S knife.

The design is manufactured by several makers, including Blackjack, Yancey and Mar. The specifications here refer to the model made by Bill Harsey, but are virtually identical in other makes.

Manufacturer:	Bill Harsey, Creswell, Oregon, USA
Model:	Applegate-Fairbairn Fighting Knife
Length overall:	11in.
Blade length:	6 1/2in.
Blade shape:	Parallel-sided blade with spear point
Blade material:	145CM stainless steel
Edge:	Double-edge bevel ground
Grip:	Moulded Lexan in waisted shape with longitudinal grooves and lanyard hole; separate double guard
Construction:	Handle screwed to full length tang
Features:	Lead weights in handle adjustable for balance

The Blue Devil is a specialised sleeve dagger intended to be worn concealed and deployed rapidly when needed. It is basically a single piece of steel, measuring 8in. overall, with a symmetrical 3 1/2in. dagger blade. This blade length is misleading, since the shape of the knife allows it to stab deeper than the length of the blade. The handle is formed by shaping the other end of the steel, with milled depressions for grip and finger grooves for the first finger and thumb.

The result is a thin, flat knife that may be worn in its sheath on forearm or leg without restricting movement or showing unduly through clothing. However, it can be rapidly drawn when required and provides a lethal fighting blade which can be used for stabbing or slashing.

Not a knife that would be particularly useful for field chores, but highly practical for its intended purpose, offering a larger effective blade length and better grip than many boot and concealment knives.

Manufacturer:	Blackjack Knives Ltd, Effingham, Illinois, USA
Model:	Blue Devil
Length overall:	8in.
Blade length:	3 1/2in.
Blade shape:	Spear point
Blade material:	1085 carbon steel, Rc 55-57
Edge:	Bevel-grind, double-edge
Grip:	Milled holes in plain steel tang
Construction:	One-piece steel
Sheath:	Nylon sheath designed to be worn concealed on forearm or calf

The American military knife supplier Camillus offers two sizes of boot knife which are identical in design. The standard model measures 7in. overall, with a 3 1/8in. blade, while the large model is 8 5/8in. overall and has a 4 1/2in. blade.

The blade is a symmetrical, convex, dagger shape, sharpened both sides to give a double edge. It has extended choils both sides which provide a double guard. The knife is a full tang design, with black chequered Valox scales pinned to either side to form the handle. The blade is made of 440 stainless steel, with a parkerised matt finish.

The knife comes in a black leather sheath with stainless steel boot clip.

Manufacturer:	Camillus Cutlery Co, Camillus, New York, USA
Model:	CM-CP75 Boot Knife
Length overall:	7in. (large version 8 5/8in. overall)
Blade length:	3 1/8in. (large version 4 1/2in.)
Blade shape:	Double-edged, spear point
Blade material:	440 stainless steel with parkerized matt finish
Edge:	Bevel grind
Grip:	Black chequered Valox scales; guard formed from extended choils
Construction:	Scales pinned to full tang
Sheath:	Black leather sheath with boot clip

Based on the traditional Scottish skean dhu, the Cold Steel Culloden measures 8 1/2in. overall and has a 5in. serrated edge with a 1 3/4in. jimped section on the back edge which provides extra purchase for the thumb or forefinger. The blade is sharply pointed but ground on one edge only. True to type, there is no guard, and the handle is waisted and has a flared pommel. The handle is made from moulded Kraton rubber, with a pin (with decorated head) holding it to the full-length tang. Two versions are available: in stainless steel and in carbon V steel. An attractive piece which combines a traditional design with modern materials, this knife nevertheless has considerable limitations, both as a fighter and as a general purpose tool.

Manufacturer:	Cold Steel Inc, Ventura, California, USA
Model:	11SS Culloden
Length overall:	8 1/2in.
Blade length:	5in.
Blade shape:	Single-edged convex curve to sharply-angled point
Blade material:	400 series stainless steel (carbon steel version also available)
Edge:	Hollow ground with serrations on main edge, and 1 3/4in. jimped section on back edge
Grip:	Chequered, black Kraton rubber handle in traditional waisted pattern with flared pommel
Construction:	Handle riveted to tang; no guard
Sheath:	Cordura belt sheath

The Cold Steel Peacekeeper I is a double-edged dagger measuring 12in. overall, and with a 6 1/2in. spear point blade. The blade - which is available in either stainless or carbon V steel - has its widest part about one-third of its length back from the tip. This gives excellent penetration and also provides a slight reverse curve cutting edge; making this a superb fighter well suited to stabbing and slashing. The handle is black Kraton moulded in a coffin shape and chequered for extra grip. The double guard is moulded with the handle and is radiused at the base, making this a particularly comfortable knife to use. The double edge limits this knife's usefulness for general camp chores, but there is no doubt that it excels as a pure fighter. In the circumstances, the name 'Peacekeeper' has an ironic ring to it.

Manufacturer:	Cold Steel Inc., Ventura, California, USA
Model:	10D Peacekeeper I
Length overall:	12in.
Blade length:	6 1/2in.
Blade shape:	Spear point
Blade material:	Stainless steel and carbon steel versions available
Edge:	Double-edged, hollow-ground
Grip:	Symmetrical, chequered, black, Kraton rubber, one-piece handle incorporating double guard and lanyard hole
Construction:	Handle moulded to full-length tang
Sheath:	Black Cordura sheath with leg tie

Cold Steel's Peacekeeper II is a smaller version of the Peacekeeper I. All the comments made about the Peacekeeper I apply equally to this model, with the proviso that the smaller and lighter blade will be marginally less effective at both stabbing and slashing. Still a highly effective fighting knife, however, and one that comes with a boot clip sheath so it can be worn semi-concealed.

Manufacturer:	Cold Steel Inc., Ventura, California, USA
Model:	10B Peacekeeper II
Length overall:	9 3/4in.
Blade length:	5 1/4in.
Blade shape:	Spear point
Blade material:	Stainless steel and carbon steel versions available
Edge:	Double-edged, hollow-ground
Grip:	Symmetrical, chequered, black, Kraton rubber, one-piece handle incorporating double guard and lanyard hole
Construction:	Handle moulded to full-length tang
Sheath:	Black Cordura sheath with boot clip

The Delta Dart is a particularly nasty or useful weapon, depending on one's point of view. Made entirely of Zytel glass-reinforced nylon, it has no metal parts and so is extremely hard to detect with conventional search aids such as X-ray equipment and magnetometers. Its 8in. length can be readily concealed in clothing or on the person, and even when held ready for use it does not catch the eye in the same way as a conventional knife blade.

Skilfully used, however, the dart is as lethal as any knife. Its blade is triangular in cross-section and comes to a very sharp point. It is not suitable for slashing, but penetrates deeply, even through clothing. The rounded pommel allows it to be held between the second and the third finger, in the manner of a push dagger, allowing much deeper penetration.

The triangular blade shape leaves a particularly serious wound which tends to remain open, causing rapid blood loss. A puncture in the abdomen will allow air to be sucked into the chest cavity, collapsing the lungs. If the victim survives, the wound is difficult to treat and does not heal easily.

Manufacturer:	Special Projects Division, Cold Steel Inc., Ventura, California, USA
Model:	92DD Delta Dart
Length overall:	8in.
Blade length:	3 1/2in.
Blade shape:	Triangular-section spear point
Blade material:	Zytel glass-reinforced nylon
Edge:	Moulded
Grip:	Round section, chequered Zytel with rounded pommel
Construction:	One-piece moulded
Features:	No metal parts

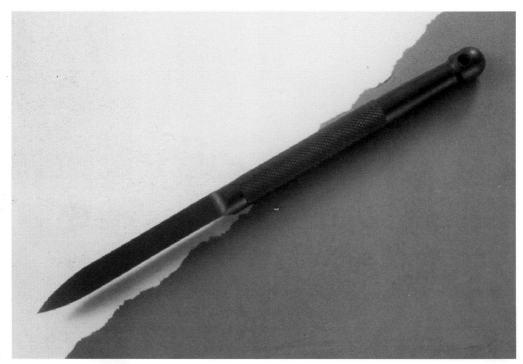

The CAT, or Covert Action Tanto, is made entirely of Zytel glass-reinforced nylon, making it difficult to detect by X-ray or magnetometer search. While the unusual materials limit its usefulness for general tasks, it still makes a highly effective weapon, with all the legendary penetrating power of the conventional steel Tanto blade. Although less easily concealed than the Delta Dart, the CAT does allow the use of a slashing stroke as well as stabbing, and offers the psychological advantage of having an appearance just as intimidating as a conventional knife.

Manufacturer:	Special Projects Division, Cold Steel Inc., Ventura, California, USA
Model:	92CAT Tanto
Length overall:	11 1/in.
Blade length:	5 3/4in.
Blade shape:	Tanto
Blade material:	Zytel glass-reinforced nylon
Edge:	Bevel ground with chisel tip
Grip:	Oval section, chequered Zytel handle with integral single guard and lanyard hole
Construction:	One-piece moulded
Features:	No metal parts

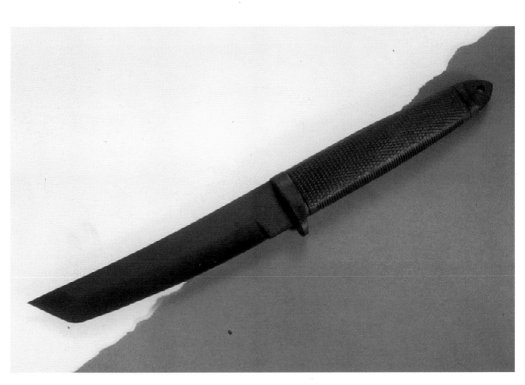

The Tai Pan from Cold Steel measures 13in. overall, it has a broad, straight-sided, double-edged 7 1/8in. dagger blade with a spear point which is effective for stabbing, slashing and hacking at an opponent. The handle is similar to the Tanto - a tapering oval-section handle covered with chequered black Kraton rubber, with a stainless steel double guard, bolster and pommel. The knife is completely symmetrical, and can be used either way up in the hand.

The Tai Pan is similar in many ways to the Applegate Fairbairn fighting knife. Although capable of being used for general chores, the Tai Pan is primarily a fighting knife and excels for this purpose.

Manufacturer:	Cold Steel Inc., Ventura, California, USA
Model:	13D Tai Pan
Length overall:	13in.
Blade length:	7 1/8in.
Blade shape:	Spear point
Blade material:	8A stainless steel
Edge:	Double-edged, hollow-ground
Grip:	Round, tapered, chequered, black Kraton rubber, one-piece handle, brushed stainless guard and pommel with lanyard hole
Construction:	Handle moulded to full-length tang
Sheath:	Black leather belt sheath

The unique characteristics of the Tanto design make it particularly useful as a fighter, and it is preferred by some exponents to the more familiar dagger and Bowie-style blades.

The Tanto blade shape was developed in the Far East to pierce metal body armour and its penetrating power is legendary. The angled chisel point pierces amazingly well through all types of material - several Cold Steel catalogues show the blade pushed through a car door from the outside, for instance, having penetrated the sheet steel of the door panel.

The 6in. stainless steel blade is single-edged, with the full thickness of the steel retained almost to the tip for extra strength. The main edge is almost straight, and the blade has a slight upsweep towards the tip.

The grip consists of a tapering oval-section handle covered with chequered black Kraton rubber, with a stainless steel, single guard, bolster and pommel. The pommel incorporates a lanyard hole, and comes to a point which can also be used against an opponent, by bringing it down on his skull.

Manufacturer:	Cold Steel Inc., Ventura, California, USA
Model:	13BN Master Tanto San Mai
Length overall:	11 1/4in.
Blade length:	6in.
Blade shape:	Tanto
Blade material:	San Mai III steel
Edge:	Bevel-ground with chisel tip
Grip:	Round section, tapered, chequered, black Kraton rubber, one-piece handle, brushed stainless single guard, and pommel with lanyard hole
Construction:	Handle moulded to full-length tang
Sheath:	Black leather belt sheath

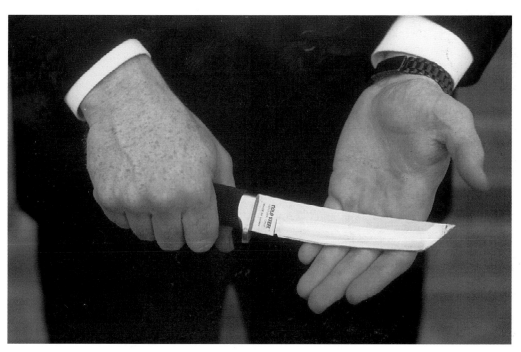

The Recon Tanto is a development of Cold Steel's standard Tanto design, which matches the proven effectiveness of the Tanto blade shape with a Westernised grip shape and black powder coated Carbon V steel blade.

The blade of the Recon Tanto is 7in. long, giving an overall length of 11 3/4in. The coating helps to protect the steel from the elements, as well as avoiding the reflections of the brightly polished stainless steel of the standard Tanto. This might reduce the psychological effect of a flashing blade in certain situations, but is a positive advantage in covert and night-time operations.

The grip is a single piece moulded from black Kraton rubber and incorporates a single guard. It is more rectangular in cross-section than the more traditional Tanto type, which helps the user to keep track of the knife's position, as well as to resist any twisting of the knife in the hand.

Manufacturer:	Cold Steel Inc., Ventura, California, USA
Model:	13RT Recon Tanto
Length overall:	11 1/4in.
Blade length:	7in.
Blade shape:	Tanto
Blade material:	Black coated Carbon V steel
Edge:	Bevel-ground with chisel tip
Grip:	Chequered, black Kraton rubber, one-piece handle with integral single guard, and lanyard hole
Construction:	Handle moulded to full-length tang
Sheath:	Black Cordura belt sheath

The Colt Black Diamond series is advertised as 'the ultimate in knife technology... a perfect back-up tool for military, police, swat, customs inspectors and other law enforcement personnel.' These knives certainly make use of modern materials and manufacturing methods, with 6 1/8in. 420 J2 stainless steel blades and handles that combine grey Zytel with black Kraton rubber for strength, comfort and a sure grip.

The handle is based on a solid 'interframe' of Zytel with a recess for the full length tang. The tang has a hole at the end which matches up with a corresponding hole in the Zytel piece; a stainless steel tube is driven through to anchor the interframe firmly to the tang. This construction gives strength and rigidity and the softer Kraton rubber provides a comfortable hold. Ridges and chequered panels of Zytel show through the rubber, giving the handle a distinctive look as well as providing added grip.

The Black Diamond series offers three blade options: a double-edged dagger with central fuller, a spear point design based on the M7 bayonet, and a Tanto shape. Also available for these knives is a lightweight, black nylon, shoulder harness and sheath which allows the knife to be worn concealed under a jacket or coat. Removed from the harness, the sheath has a stainless steel clip that can be attached to a boot or belt. Alternatively, there is a black leather sheath with a belt loop and press-stud, quick-release strap. It is a versatile system that enables the knife to be worn in a number of different ways - overtly or concealed - to suit the user's requirements.

Manufacturer:	United Cutlery, Sevierville, Tennessee, USA
Model:	CT8 Black Diamond Liberator
Length overall:	10 3/4in.
Blade length:	6 1/8in.
Blade shape:	Dagger blade with fuller (also available: tanto and bayonet type blades)
Blade material:	3/16in. thick 420 stainless steel
Edge:	Bevel-grind
Grip:	Solid grey Zytel with chequered panels and black Kraton partial covering
Construction:	Zytel interframe pinned to full-length tang by stainless steel lanyard tube
Sheath:	Black leather belt sheath. Shoulder harness and black nylon sheath with boot/belt clip also available

The origins of the Combat Smatchet may be traced back to Celtic short swords, but the modern design is attributed to Colonel Rex Applegate and Captain WE Fairbairn. Applegate worked for the Office of Strategic Services during the Second World War, while Fairbairn was one of the designers of the Fairbairn Sykes Fighting Knife used during the War by British Commandos. A single-edged smatchet was issued to OSS operatives in Europe.

In his wartime classic *All-In Fighting*, Captain Fairbairn says of the Smatchet: 'The psychological reaction of any man, when he first takes the smatchet in his hand, is full justification for its recommendation as a fighting weapon. He will immediately register all the essential qualities of a good soldier - confidence, determination and aggressiveness.' His recommended blows with the smatchet include driving the point into an enemy's stomach, chopping to the neck, wrist or arm to sever the main arteries, and smashing the pommel into the face.

In combat, the smatchet is very effective for stabbing, hacking and slashing. Its weight and blade shape create deep, debilitating wounds with the minimum of effort. Although ostensibly a close-quarter combat weapon, the smatchet is also effective as a general-purpose camp and survival tool; it may be used for chopping, digging and even paddling a raft or canoe.

The blade is a broad leaf shape, with a spear point. It measures 10in. long, and 3in. wide at its widest point. The blade has serrated sections on either edge for more effective cutting of difficult materials such as rope and webbing. There is a hole drilled through the blade near the guard, so that one may identify the edges even in total darkness by feel. This allows one to use one side as a 'working edge' and keep the other razor sharp for emergency use.

Several manufacturers offer a version of the Combat Smatchet, including Bill Harsey and Wells Creek Knife & Gun Works of Oregon, USA. The model shown here, and described in the specifications, is by Al Mar.

Manufacturer: Al Mar Knives Inc., Lake Oswego, Oregon, USA

Model: Combat Smatchet

Length overall: 15in.

Blade length: 10in.

Blade shape: Wide leaf shape with spear point

Blade material: T425 stainless steel, Rc 54-56

Edge: Bevel-ground

Grip: Black Lexan plastic with longitudinal grooves and
              lanyard hole

Construction: Handle pinned to full-length tang

Sheath: Black leather sheath with leg tie

The Boot Knife from John Ek is a post-war design incorporating all the characteristics which have made Ek knives some of the most highly regarded by servicemen - a full tang, cord-wrapped design, a thick, strong blade of surgical stainless steel, and a reinforced spear point.

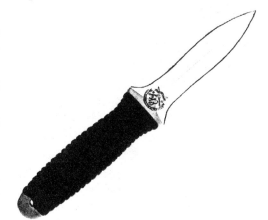

The Boot Knife is the smallest of the Ek knives and is designed to be carried covertly as a back-up weapon, in a black leather boot-clip sheath. It measures 7 1/2in. overall, with a 3 1/2in. blade with the distinctive waisted shape that is seen in other Ek blades. The waisted blade aids deep penetration when used for stabbing and provides a reverse curve edge for efficient cutting.

The Boot Knife is of simple design, being basically a single piece of steel shaped to provide blade and handle. The grip is formed from a six-foot length of black military paracord wrapped around the handle. This provides a secure and comfortable grip, and may be unwrapped for emergency use if necessary, leaving the knife fully functional although slightly less comfortable to hold.

Manufacturer:	Ek Commando Knife Co., Richmond, Virginia, USA
Model:	Ek Boot Knife
Length overall:	7 1/2in.
Blade length:	3 1/2in.
Blade shape:	Spear point, waisted
Blade material:	High carbon, surgical stainless steel
Edge:	Double-edge bevel-grind
Grip:	Paracord
Construction:	One-piece steel with 6ft. of black military specification parachute cord wrapped around tang
Sheath:	Black leather sheath with boot clip and tie holes

The Ek Warrior is the modern version of the legendary Commando Combat knife developed in the Second World War by John Ek. This knife is conservatively estimated to have sold 100,000 to American servicemen during the Second World War, and continued to be a popular private military purchase through the Korean and Vietnam wars.

The Ek knife is a highly functional design, with no frills. It is built around a single piece of thick steel, with a tang the full width and length of the handle. This makes the knife exceptionally strong - far stronger than a 'rat tail' or partial-length tang. The grips are made of contoured hardwood scales, riveted through the tang, and the tang extends beyond the grips to provide a round ended 'skull crusher' pommel (a more pointed pommel might appear more effective, but would endanger the user when carried in a sheath). This pommel may also be used for prying and hammering.

The blade is bevel-ground to a waisted spear point shape, with the back edge on this model extending roughly half way along the length of the blade (Bowie blade model illustrated). The spear point is very strong and provides excellent penetration for stabbing, while the waisted shape helps the blade to penetrate deeper into the opponent's body.

The knife balances well in the hand, and may be held in a variety of grips for different fighting styles and strokes.

Manufacturer:	Ek Commando Knife Co., Richmond, Virginia, USA
Model:	Warrior
Length overall:	12 1/2in.
Blade length:	6 5/8in.
Blade shape:	Spear point, waisted
Blade material:	High carbon stainless steel, with sandblasted non-reflective finish
Edge:	Bevel-ground
Grip:	Wood, with extended tang forming 'skull crusher' pommel
Construction:	Wood handles secured to full-size tang by three large rivets
Sheath:	Nylon web sheath

The Ek Paragrip range of knives have the same distinguished history and rugged design as the Ek Commando knives, but with paracord wrapped around the full-size tang to provide the grip in place of the riveted wood scales of the Commando models.

The paracord can be unwrapped if required, to provide 18ft. of military specification cord which is enormously versatile and useful for all manner of jobs in a survival situation. With the paracord removed, the knife is fully functional, the only drawback being a slightly less comfortable grip.

Ek Paragrip models come in a range of blade shapes, including part double-edged and full double-edged spear points, and a clip point Bowie design. The knives are around 12 1/2in. long overall, with a 6 5/8in. blade. The paracord may be black or green, and the knives are available with black or green nylon web sheaths.

Manufacturer:	Ek Commando Knife Co., Richmond, Virginia, USA
Model:	S/F 3, 4, 5 and SWAT 4 and 5
Length overall:	12 1/2in.
Blade length:	6 5/8in.
Blade shape:	Spear point, waisted, or Bowie-style clip point
Blade material:	High carbon, surgical stainless steel
Edge:	Bevel-grind
Grip:	Paracord, black or green
Construction:	One-piece steel with 18ft. of military specification parachute cord wrapped around tang
Sheath:	Nylon web sheath, black or green

The legendary Fairbairn-Sykes is perhaps the most widely known military knife of all time, a classic that has become synonymous with daring Second World War Commando raids and still adorns the cap badges and insignia of elite British units.

The Commandos were formed in 1940 to 'carry out raids... to destroy enemy installations and obtain information'. Captains Fairbairn and Sykes had served with the Shanghai Municipal Police and were experienced in martial arts and hand-to-hand combat. They were put in charge of teaching close-combat fighting skills at the Commando Basic Training Centre at Achnacarry in Scotland.

Fairbairn and his colleagues in Shanghai had worked on fighting knife designs, modifying British bayonets. For the Commandos they wanted a knife that was grip-heavy, and could be held in the fencing position. This is why the F-S knife handle is bottle-shaped - it is based on fencing foil designs. The grip is shaped to fall into the natural crease between the palm and the ball of the thumb, with the narrow neck of the grip fitting against the ball of the hand and the thumb and index finger grasping the forward part of the grip.

The double-edged tapered dagger blade is intended to provide excellent penetration for stabbing, but with two good edges for slashing. The full length tang gives good strength to the knife.

Sykes taught that the knife should be used delicately, 'as an artist uses his paint brush', making incisions with almost surgical precision. Fairbairn's wartime book, *All-In Fighting*, describes with anatomical detail the positions of the brachial, radial, carotid and subclavian arteries, and the techniques by which these may be cut with the F-S knife. A table details the depth of the arteries below the surface, and the length of time a man will take to lose consciousness when each one is cut.

During the War years, the original First Model F-S knife was developed, both to increase its effectiveness and to speed production with the materials and manufacturing technology available in wartime Britain. The early 3in. S-shaped guard was reduced to 2in. in production models to make it less likely to snag in clothing, and later became straight rather than S-shaped. Early examples have a ricasso or flat to the blade close to the hilt; more common, later F-S knives are bevelled all the way to the hilt. The grip was originally made of lathe-turned brass and chequered for added grip. As brass was needed for shell casings, this was replaced in the Third Model by a die-cast, zinc alloy handle, with rings for grip.

An enormous number of variations on the F-S design were produced by official and unofficial makers, some of which are highly prized by modern collectors. Genuine wartime F-S knives command a premium, and many

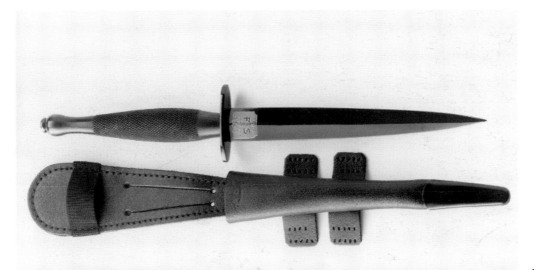

replicas and deliberate fakes have been produced since - so collectors should take care to ensure they know the true history of any example they are thinking of purchasing.

Manufacturer: British War Office contractors

Model: Fairbairn-Sykes Fighting Knife, Third Model

Length overall: 11 5/8in.

Blade length: 7in.

Blade shape: Tapered diagonal-section dagger blade

Blade material: Carbon steel

Edge: Bevel-ground

Grip: Cast zinc alloy, ringed, with characteristic bottle shape

Construction: Full-length, rat-tail type tang, with rounded nut at pommel screwed on to threaded end of tang

Sheath: Brown leather sheath with metal chape, belt loop and tabs for attachment to clothing or equipment, and black elastic strap to hold knife in position

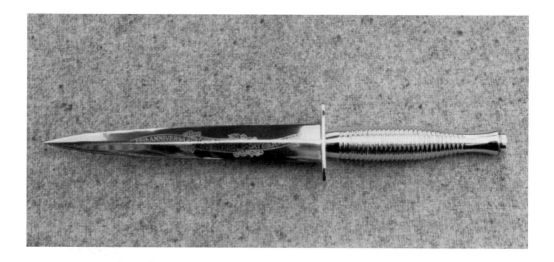

Gerber's Guardian Back-Up is a small boot knife which manages to combine small size and concealability with an effective fighting blade. The knife measures 7 1/4in. overall, with a 3 3/8in. blade of high carbon stainless steel. The blade is a double-edged tapered dagger shape, rather like a foreshortened Fairbairn-Sykes. It is bevel-ground to a sharp point, and finished with a black powder coating which matches the black handle. The handle is made of black Santoprene rubber with integral double guard and a textured surface for improved grip. There is a grooved portion at each edge of the grip, and a thumb recess on either side just behind the hilt. The butt is flared slightly.

As a pure fighting knife, the Guardian is rather small, but then it is designed to be used as a concealed last resort defensive weapon, and its small size is part of that concept.

The sheath is part of the system, and consists of a rigid, moulded black plastic unit with a stainless steel clip that may be reversed to permit the knife to be worn either way up on belt or boot. Slots in the sheath also allow it to be strapped to the user's arm, leg or equipment. The sheath features an adjustable retention system which holds the edges of the double guard. Sliding buttons may be set to hold the knife relatively loosely, to allow easy withdrawal, or tightly for security - or any position in between. A hole at the tip of the sheath serves both as a drain hole and to allow a leg tie to be fitted.

Having used this knife, I may say that the sheath works very effectively, and the knife itself balances well in the hand and is more effective than its size might suggest. My only complaint is that the sheath is inclined to be noisy, when one withdraws or inserts the knife, and if it knocks against other equipment.

Manufacturer:	Gerber (a division of Fiskars Inc.), Portland, Oregon, USA
Model:	Guardian Back-Up
Length overall:	7 1/4in.
Blade length:	3 3/8in.
Blade shape:	Dagger
Blade material:	0.156in. thick, high carbon stainless steel, with black epoxy coated finish
Edge:	Double, bevel-ground
Grip:	Grooved and textured Santoprene rubber
Construction:	Santoprene grip moulded on to full-size tang
Sheath:	Rigid black plastic sheath with adjustable tension locking system and belt/boot clip

The Gerber Mk I was actually developed after the Mk II, and was designed in conjunction with military-knife-fighting experts during the Vietnam War. The Mk I shares the basic shape and concept of the Applegate Fairbairn fighting knife, with its tapered dagger-shaped blade, forward-angled double guard, and oval-section handle which is fattest in the centre of the palm.

The Mk I is 8 3/4in. overall, with a 4 3/4in. 440A stainless steel blade which can be supplied bright or epoxy-coated black. The handle is made of cast aluminium with a black epoxy finish with a non-slip texture. The butt is slightly flared and has a lanyard hole.

The Mk I is a serious, no-frills fighting knife. It is a little shorter than some would prefer (hence the alternative of the Mk II), but is well balanced and an efficient and effective fighting tool.

Manufacturer:	Gerber (a division of Fiskars Inc.), Portland, Oregon, USA
Model:	Mk I
Length overall:	8 3/4in.
Blade length:	4 3/4in.
Blade shape:	Dagger
Blade material:	1/4in. thick, 15/16in. wide 440A stainless steel, Rc 57-59. Finish either satin or black epoxy-coated
Edge:	Double, bevel-ground
Grip:	Cast aluminium, contoured, incorporating double guard, textured black epoxy-coated, with lanyard hole
Construction:	Guard and handle formed as one piece
Sheath:	Black Cordura belt sheath with leg tie loop

Developed during the Vietnam War with the advice of military-knife-fighting experts, the Mk II is a development of the Fairbairn-Sykes concept of a fighting dagger. A no-frills design, it has a 6 1/2in. blade made of 1/4in. thick 440A stainless steel, hardened to Rc 57-59. The blade is a parallel-sided dagger type, with a strong spear point and a serrated section on each edge for extra cutting power. This blade is excellent for stabbing, slashing, ripping and cutting, making the Mk II a highly effective fighting weapon.

The handle is a single aluminium casting, incorporating a double guard and contoured to fit the hand well. It has a truncated cone pommel which may be used as a 'skull crusher'.

Manufacturer:	Gerber (a division of Fiskars Inc.), Portland, Oregon, USA
Model:	Mk II
Length overall:	11 1/2in.
Blade length:	6 1/2in.
Blade shape:	Dagger, with serrated sections near hilt
Blade material:	1/4in. thick 440A stainless steel, Rc 57-59. Finish either satin or black epoxy coated
Edge:	Double, bevel-ground, with serrated section
Grip:	Cast aluminium incorporating double guard, black epoxy-coated, with lanyard hole
Construction:	Double guard and handle formed as one piece
Sheath:	Black Cordura belt sheath with leg tie

The Sleeve Dagger is one of the notorious weapons of clandestine operations during the Second World War. It is basically a steel spike, made of a single piece of stainless steel. Measuring 7in. long overall, it has a 3 1/2in. 'blade' ground into a triangular section culminating in a sharp spear point. The three flats of the blade have deep fullers or 'blood grooves'. The edges of the blade are sharpened, although because of the blade profile they cannot be as sharp as a normal knife blade.

Stabbing with the triangular blade creates a devastating wound which allows rapid blood loss and does not heal easily (see also Cold Steel Special Projects Delta Dart). Although the blade can also be used for slashing, it is less effective than a knife and is best used for stabbing.

The handle is rectangular in section, with rounded edges, measuring 3/8in. wide and 1/4in. thick. The butt is grooved just before the end forming a hammer head which may be used to deliver a blow.

The Sleeve Dagger is carried in a brown leather sheath which has a strap to hold it to the forearm or leg, where it can be worn concealed but drawn quickly when needed.

Manufacturer:	HG Long & Co., Sheffield, England
Model:	OSS Sleeve Dagger
Length overall:	7in.
Blade length:	3 1/2in.
Blade shape:	Triangular cross-section spike with fullers ground into flats
Blade material:	Stainless steel with sandblasted, non-reflective finish
Edge:	Sharpened spike point. The three edges are also sharp
Grip:	Bare steel
Construction:	Machined from one piece of steel
Sheath:	Leather sheath with strap for wear on forearm, concealed by sleeve

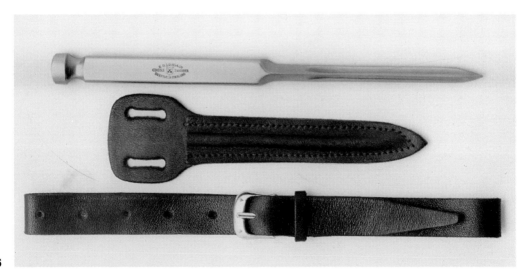

The Smith & Wesson Military Model Boot Knife is basically a miniature version of the Combat Smatchet - comparison of the photograph of this knife with those of the Smatchet earlier in this chapter will show the obvious similarity. Like the Smatchet, the S&W Boot Knife has a broad, symmetrical, leaf-shaped blade ending in a spear point. It has a similar handle, with longitudinal grooves for grip and integral, forward-angled, double guard. There is a hole in the ricasso to identify the 'working' edge, even by feel in the dark.

The dimensions are much smaller, however - the S&W Boot Knife measures 9 3/4in. overall, with a 5in. blade (compared with the massive 10in. blade of the Smatchet). This gives the Boot Knife completely different handling characteristics - it balances and handles much more like a conventional knife. The Smatchet blade shape still has certain advantages even at this size, however. It still offers what is effectively a reverse curve cutting edge, and the spear point is immensely strong.

The blade shape keeps much of the weight forward, giving better chopping performance than one might expect from such a relatively short blade.

This is one of a number of 'mini-Smatchets' offered by different makers, including Harsey and Mar. These models are in effect a variation on the Applegate-Fairbairn Fighting Knife design, bringing some of the advantages of the Smatchet blade shape to this highly effective fighter.

Manufacturer:	Smith & Wesson, Springfield, MA, USA
Model:	Military Model Boot Knife
Length overall:	9 3/4in.
Blade length:	5in.
Blade shape:	Smatchet
Blade material:	440 stainless steel
Edge:	Double-edged, bevel-ground
Grip:	Moulded black Kraton rubber with longitudinal grooves
Construction:	Handle screwed to full-length tang
Sheath:	Black leather boot clip sheath

SOG's Desert Dagger was developed in response to military personnel needs, and aims to provide a more versatile tool than the regular dagger-type fighting knife. It has a typical dagger-type blade, with parallel sides and a strong spear point, but with the addition of a central fuller or 'blood groove', and two types of serrated edge for a short section on either side - fine serrations on one side, and larger, deeper serrations on the other. The knife also has an enlarged, flat-ended, stainless steel pommel which may be used for hammering in the field.

The grip is of Kraton rubber, contoured and with chequering for extra grip. One notable feature of this knife is the soldered crossguard, something that is generally found only on the most expensive knives.

Whether the different serration types are really needed is debatable, but there is no doubt that this is a serious fighting knife, and one that is also capable of taking on a range of general chores in the field.

Manufacturer:	SOG Knives, Edmonds, Washington, USA
Model:	Desert Dagger
Length overall:	12in.
Blade length:	6 1/2in.
Blade shape:	Parallel-edged, dagger blade with spear point
Blade material:	0.18in. thick 440A stainless steel, Rc 57-58
Edge:	Double, bevel-ground, with fuller and serrated sections on both edges near hilt
Grip:	One-piece Kraton grip, with all-round chequering. Flat steel pommel suitable for hammering.
Construction:	Full tang, with soldered crossguard
Sheath:	Black nylon belt sheath with leg tie

Designed as a back-up weapon for law enforcement personnel, the Pentagon has a 5in. tapered dagger blade with one plain edge and one serrated. The waisted handle is made of Kraton, with chequering for grip. There is no guard as such, the bolster fitting flush with the handle. There are thumb notches on either side of the ricasso, so the knife can be used equally well with the serrated or the plain edge uppermost.

The Pentagon comes with a black leather boot clip sheath with press studded retaining strap.

Manufacturer: SOG Knives, Edmonds, Washington, USA

Model: Pentagon

Length overall: 9 3/4in.

Blade length: 5in.

Blade shape: Tapered dagger

Blade material: 0.16in. thick 440-A stainless steel, Rc 56-57

Edge: Double, bevel-ground, with one edge serrated

Grip: One-piece flared Kraton grip, with all-round chequering

Construction: Full tang

Sheath: Black leather scabbard with boot/belt clip

Although not a current design, this knife is included here since it illustrates a type of fighting knife which still influences some modern designers and is still manufactured in reproduction form and therefore may be encountered in certain theatres of operation.

The Trench Knife is a particularly versatile weapon, combining not just a blade but also a heavy brass knuckle-duster and a pointed steel 'skull crusher'. The loops of the knuckle-duster have points to make a blow more damaging.

The modern reproduction of this First World War knife measures 11in. overall, with a 6 1/2in. polished blade of stainless steel. The handle is cast brass and is held in place by a threaded nut which screws on to the end of the full-length tang. The nut is hexagonal at the base and is extended into a point to form the 'skull crusher' pommel spike.

All in all, this is a crude but effective weapon, well suited to hand-to-hand fighting in confined spaces.

Manufacturer:	Replica distributed by United Cutlery, Sevierville, Tennessee, USA
Model:	WWI Trench Knife
Length overall:	11in.
Blade length:	6 1/2in.
Blade shape:	Dagger
Blade material:	5/32in. thick 420 J2 stainless steel
Edge:	Bevel-ground
Grip:	Solid brass one-piece handle incorporating guard and knuckle duster, with conical 'skull crusher' pommel
Construction:	Full-length tang
Sheath:	Metal sheath with non-glare black finish

BAYONETS

The Kalashnikov assault rifle in its various forms (AK47, AK74 and derivatives) remains the standard infantry weapon of former Communist bloc states and their allies. Consequently, the corresponding bayonet is still in widespread service, and may be encountered in just about any part of the world, whether in the hands of government troops or rebel and guerrilla forces.

The bayonet has been manufactured in several countries over the years, and a number of minor variations exist which are significant to collectors but have little relevance here. Suffice it to say that most examples are substantially the same in materials, design and dimensions.

The AK47 bayonet is a relatively crude but effective tool. Measuring 11in. overall, it has a 6in. clip point blade, with a serrated sawback edge. There is an oval hole in the blade which engages a knob on the scabbard, to form a scissor-type wire cutter. The steel sheath often has a latex grip to provide electrical insulation, so that the cutters may be used to breach electrified wire obstacles.

The bayonet's handle is formed from moulded plastic grip scales, fixed to the tang with machine screws. The guard is extended to form a muzzle ring, which fits around the rifle's muzzle. At the butt end is a clip with a catch mechanism which engages on a protrusion beneath the barrel of the Kalashnikov rifle. This attaches the bayonet firmly to the rifle until the catch is released with the push-button. The bayonet typically has a thin webbing strap which extends from the guard to the butt.

This bayonet is conceived as a multi-purpose combat knife which will be useful to soldiers for many chores in the field, as well as for hand-to-hand fighting and use as a bayonet when necessary. Like most multi-purpose tools, it does an adequate job of most tasks, but does not really excel in any one. As a general purpose field knife, however, it is hard to beat.

Manufacturer:	Former Communist bloc state factories
Model:	Bayonet, AK47
Length overall:	11in.
Blade length:	6in.
Blade shape:	Clip point, Bowie-type
Blade material:	Stainless steel, Rc 56-58
Edge:	Bevel-ground
Grip:	Black or brown plastic scales with chequered pattern
Construction:	Scales attached to tang with machine screws; butt incorporates clip to attach to fitting on Kalashnikov assault rifle and derivatives
Sheath:	Steel sheath with attachment for bayonet blade to form scissor-type wire cutter

A Eickhorn GmbH are one of the leading manufacturers of military knives in the world and supply bayonets and combat knives to a number of NATO armies. Their leading bayonet/combat knife system is the KCB 77 - a modular system which allows a government to specify the features and fittings to meet its requirements in a combat knife or bayonet.

The example shown here is the USM9, a bayonet which at first glance resembles the AK47 design with its clip point blade, rectangular section handle, and rigid sheath that combines with the bayonet to form a scissors-type wire cutter.

There is much more to this bayonet than meets the eye, however. Quite apart from the stringent testing and quality control employed by Eickhorn, the USM9 has a number of additional features which add to its usefulness in the field.

For instance, the knife and bayonet are electrically insulated, and the knife handle incorporates a voltage tester that will illuminate a small bulb if the blade touches an electrified conductor. This warns the soldier that the fence or obstacle he is facing is electrified.

The guard is hooked forward to form a bottle opener, which may also be used for various prying and levering tasks. The catch has a lubrication point, which applies a small squirt of grease to the moving parts each time the bayonet is fitted or removed from the rifle. There is a protective cap to keep the catch free of dirt and debris when the bayonet is not attached to the rifle.

The scabbard may be unclipped from its nylon webbing hanger, so that the wire cutters can be quickly deployed without the soldier removing his webbing. On the back of the scabbard is a sapphire sharpening stone. The scabbard has an adjustable retaining spring to hold the bayonet blade in place; this can be set to release easily if the bayonet may be needed in a hurry, or screwed down tightly so that vigorous activity will not dislodge the bayonet.

A plastic cap protects the wire cutter end of the scabbard. This is not only to prevent the wire cutter from snagging in clothing or undergrowth, but also allows the bayonet in its scabbard to be used as a baton (with the retaining system adjusted to its tightest position), for example, for riot control or by military police. For riot control, an 80,000-volt piezo-electric 'cattle prod' type attachment can be fitted to the end of the scabbard, and used either in the hand or attached to a rifle.

Altogether, the KCB 77 is a versatile and well-thought-out system which effectively meets the needs of modern soldiers

Manufacturer:	Eickhorn GmbH, Solingen, Germany
Model:	USM9 (KCB 77 system)
Length overall:	11 11/16in.
Blade length:	6 5/8in.
Blade shape:	Clip point
Blade material:	Carbon steel with corrosion-resistant black finish
Edge:	Bevel-ground
Grip:	Ribbed and contoured plastic scales, rectangular section, incorporating voltage tester
Construction:	Scales fitted to full-length tang; extended guard forms muzzle ring; catch in butt fits to rifle
Sheath:	Sophisticated rigid plastic sheath with multiple features, including wire cutter, screwdriver tip, adjustable tension blade retention and clip attachment to belt hanger. Optional accessories include protective end cap and 'cattle prod' attachment for riot control

Eickhorn's USM series is based on the M7 design, but is available in a variety of configurations to fit almost any military rifle in use today, including the M16 A1 and A2, FN-FAL, SIG and H&K G3. The basic blade shape is a parallel-sided dagger with spear point. Handles are of moulded plastic (glassfibre-reinforced polyamide), contoured to fit the hand and chequered for grip. The handles are fixed to the tang with machine screws. Muzzle rings and butt catches vary to suit the particular rifle the bayonet is intended for.

Eickhorn take pride in the quality of their materials and manufacturing methods, and their USM series, used by a number of NATO armies, is no exception. Components undergo rigorous testing for strength, resilience, hardness and other characteristics, under extreme conditions of temperature and humidity. The knives and scabbards are insulated against high voltage electricity and are tested for resistance to fungal growth, corrosion and chemical agents.

Manufacturer:	Eickhorn GmbH, Solingen, Germany
Model:	USM 4, 5, 6, 7
Length overall:	11 11/16in.
Blade length:	6 5/8in.
Blade shape:	Spear point
Blade material:	Carbon steel, with corrosion-resistant black finish
Edge:	Bevel-ground
Grip:	Moulded plastic, contoured shape with chequering
Construction:	Grip scales screwed to full-length tang
Sheath:	Rigid plastic sheath, with nylon web hanger and wire clip for attachment to military web belt. Some sheaths incorporate wire-cutter attachment and screwdriver tip

Now superseded by the M9, the M7 was the standard US Army issue bayonet for the M16 A2 assault rifle. It is a relatively simple design, measuring 11 3/4in. overall with a 7in. spear point blade. The handle is formed from black plastic grip scales, with moulded chequering, screwed to the tang. The double guard is extended one side to form a muzzle ring, and the butt incorporates a spring-loaded catch to clip on to the dovetail attachment point on the M16 rifle.

The sheath is made of plastic, with a Cordura hanger with a wire clip for attachment to a military pattern web belt.

Manufacturer:	Ontario Knife Co, Franklinville, New York, USA (also manufactured by other US Department of Defense contractors such as Camillus)
Model:	M7 Bayonet
Length overall:	11 3/4in.
Blade length:	7in.
Blade shape:	Spear point
Blade material:	Black finished carbon steel
Edge:	Bevel-grind
Grip:	Moulded black plastic with black chequering
Construction:	Grips screwed through tang. Butt and guard designed to fix to attachment points on rifle muzzle
Sheath:	Rigid plastic sheath with Cordura hanger and wire clip for attachment to military web belt

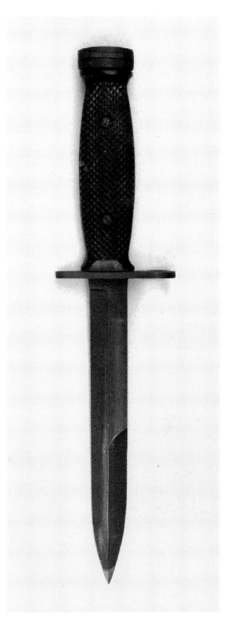

Designed as a bayonet for the M16 A2 rifle, the M9 has been adopted by the US Army and Marine Corps as well as the Australian Army, and has also proved popular with civilian users as a general field knife. Around 1995 it was estimated that Buck had produced well over 300,000 M9s for the US Army alone.

This is a hefty knife, weighing 14oz, with an overall length of 12 1/4in. and a 7 1/8in. blade of 7/32in. steel. The blade is a clip point shape, with a hollow ground main edge and a fine-toothed saw section on the back edge. On the right side of the blade is a fuller or 'blood groove'. The clip edge is partly sharpened to give a sharp point to the blade and to act as the wire cutter blade when the knife is fitted to its sheath by means of the oval hole in the blade.

As with most bayonet designs, the guard incorporates a muzzle ring, and there is a catch in the butt to attach to the appropriate fitting on the rifle.

The handle is circular in cross section and made of Zytel. It is deeply grooved and chequered to provide a sure grip even in extreme conditions. This handle may be rather hard on unprotected hands, however, and due to its circular profile may turn in the hand during use,

despite the grooves and chequering.

The knife is heavy enough for chopping and hacking, but it can also be used for more delicate work - although, as with most bayonets, the extended guard/muzzle ring makes it difficult to choke up the grip. The saw is less effective than it might appear and is better for cutting materials such as rope and webbing than for sawing wood and bone.

The rigid plastic sheath is a hefty item in its own right, weighing as much as the knife. It incorporates the wire cutter mentioned above, plus a sharpening stone and screwdriver. There is a webbing pouch that can be used for carrying small items such as a flint striker or water purification tablets. The sheath has two retaining straps for the knife, together with a retention spring inside the sheath which holds the blade. There is a Bianchi clip which allows the sheath to be attached or removed from webbing without removing other items such as water bottle and ammunition pouches which is covenient when regulations state that knives must be removed on board an aircraft, for instance.

See also Buckmaster, a combat knife based on the M9.

Manufacturer: Buck Knives, El Cajon, California, USA

Model: M9

Length overall: 12 1/4in.

Blade length: 7 1/8in.

Blade shape: Bowie-style clip point with fuller on right hand side, and serrated sawback

Blade material: 7/32in. thick forged steel, Rc 56-58. Black oxide finish available

Edge: Hollow-ground main edge, clip false edge, and serrated-type saw back

Grip: Grooved and chequered olive drab Zytel, circular section, with flared butt. Fittings for attachment to M16 A2 rifle

Construction: Tubular Zytel grip fitted over circular section handle

Sheath: Plastic and Cordura sheath incorporates sharpening stone, and fits to knife to form wire-cutters

The current British Army issue bayonet was designed specifically for the SA80 assault rifle. Like its counterparts in other armies, the SA80 bayonet is a versatile tool, capable of being used as a general purpose field knife or fighting knife when not attached to the rifle.

The blade is a clip point design, with a deep fuller or 'blood groove' on the left-hand side. The clip edge is sharpened, and the keyhole for the wire cutter is set back from this edge so that the spine of the knife acts on the wire, not the clip edge. The main edge is bevel-ground, with widely spaced serrations for the first half of its length.

The handle is unusual for a bayonet in that it is a metal tube open at both ends, designed so that the rifle's muzzle passes right through the centre. A catch on the underside at the butt end clips on to a ring on the rifle barrel to hold the bayonet in position. There are slots cut into the handle to align with the slots in the flash suppressor at the muzzle.

The scabbard is made of rigid plastic with steel fittings and has a Fastex buckle to attach to the belt hanger. It incorporates a wire-cutter attachment, with a peg that fits into a keyhole in the knife blade to form a scissors-type cutter. There is also a folding saw blade in the scabbard and a sharpening stone set into the rear face.

Manufacturer:	Royal Ordnance, UK
Model:	SA80 bayonet
Length overall:	10 3/4in.
Blade length:	7in.
Blade shape:	Clip point
Blade material:	Stainless steel
Edge:	Bevel-ground, with widely spaced serrations for first half of main edge
Grip:	Contoured hollow tubular steel handle to fit over rifle muzzle, with flash suppressor slots and attachment clip; grooves to provide extra grip
Construction:	Steel handle continuous with blade
Sheath:	Rigid plastic sheath with wire-cutter attachment, folding saw blade, and Fastex buckle attachment for belt hanger

COMBAT AND SURVIVAL KNIVES

Based on Second World War military knife designs, the Al Mar Grunt I measures 9 3/4in. overall, with a 5 1/8in. Bowie-type blade of 6A steel hardened to Rockwell 57-59. The clip of the blade is straight and ground to a false edge which extends all the way along the length of the blade to the depression just in front of the guard. This depression looks as though it could be used as a thumb rest for a 'choked-up' grip, but in fact the double guard makes this hold all but impossible.

The handle is made of stacked leather washers. The washers are threaded on to the rat-tail type tang and held in place with a pinned stainless steel butt cap. The handle thus formed is then cut to shape, including three deep grooves for added grip in wet and slippery conditions. The knife comes with a brown leather belt sheath.

This knife is a good, solid, no-frills design which is excellent for general chores, and could be used effectively as a fighter if required.

Manufacturer:	Al Mar Knives Inc., Lake Oswego, Oregon, USA
Model:	Grunt I
Length overall:	9 3/4in.
Blade length:	5 1/8in.
Blade shape:	Bowie
Blade material:	6A steel, Rc 57-59
Edge:	Deep bevel-ground with false back edge
Grip:	Grooved, stacked brown leather, with brass guard and stainless butt
Construction:	Stacked washers on full-length tang
Sheath:	Brown leather belt sheath

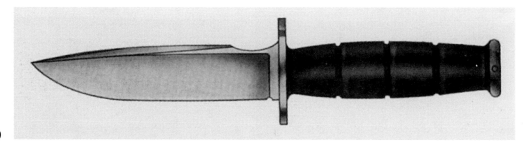

The Al Mar Grunt II is a Bowie-style fighting knife, with a long 7 3/4in. clip point blade made of 6A steel hardened to 57-59 Rc. The clip point is extended and slightly concave, giving a sharp point that penetrates exceptionally well, although there is some trade-off in tip strength: using this knife for heavy prying work would risk damaging the tip.

The blade shape makes this knife less suitable than some for general camp chores, but its length, weight and handling make it excellent for fighting - a good knife for stabbing, slashing and hacking.

Like the Grunt I, this knife has a military-style, stacked leather washer handle, with brass double guard and stainless steel butt pinned through the end of the tang. This handle is similar to that found on the USMC-type combat knifes. It provides a good chunky contoured grip that fills the hand well and is comfortable in use. The only real drawback to this type of handle is that it is round in cross-section and may turn in the hand if considerable twisting force is applied to the blade.

Manufacturer:	Al Mar Knives Inc., Lake Oswego, Oregon, USA
Model:	Grunt II
Length overall:	13in.
Blade length:	7 3/4in.
Blade shape:	Bowie with pronounced clip
Blade material:	6A steel, Rc 57-59
Edge:	Bevel-ground with sharpened clip edge
Grip:	Grooved, stacked brown leather, with brass guard and stainless butt
Construction:	Stacked washers on full-length tang
Sheath:	Brown leather belt sheath

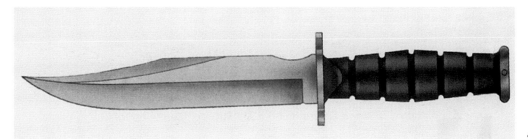

Al Mar's SERE series of knives were designed as multipurpose blades for special forces personnel (SERE stands for Survival, Evasion, Resistance, Escape). They are exceptionally good-looking knives, but immensely practical too. There are three basic models of fixed-blade knife and three folders. The fixed-blade knives are the SERE IV, SERE V and SERE VIII. The IV and V are essentially the same, except that the IV has a plain false back edge, while the V has a 2 5/8in. serrated section on the back edge. Both knives measure 10 1/2in. overall, with a deep, heavy 5 3/4in. spear point blade made of 6A steel hardened to 57-59 Rc. The model VIII is larger, at 12 1/2in. overall, with a 7in. blade.

The green micarta handles are contoured, with the lines flowing smoothly into the contoured stainless steel double guard, which has a forward-angled shape. One drawback noted by users of these knives is that the polished micarta handles offer little grip and may turn easily in the hand. This can be overcome by having the handle grooved or chequered to provide better grip.

The SERE knives are a little light for heavy chopping, but otherwise are versatile enough to tackle most field chores. They are a popular private purchase among elite military units, who recognise their value not only as a rugged and dependable field tool but also as lethally effective fighters.

Manufacturer:	Al Mar Knives Inc., Lake Oswego, Oregon, USA
Model:	SERE - Models IV, V and VIII
Length overall:	12 1/2in. (SERE VIII)
Blade length:	7in. (SERE VIII)
Blade shape:	Spear point with serrated back
Blade material:	6A steel, Rc 57-59
Edge:	Bevel-ground with false top edge and serrated back
Grip:	Green micarta; brushed stainless guard; 3 lanyard holes
Construction:	Micarta scales pinned to full tang with three hollow brass tube rivets
Sheath:	Black leather belt sheath with sharpening stone

Al Mar's SF-Sog Special Ops is an impressive fighting knife design, with an extended clip point blade. Like most of Al Mar's fixed-blade knives, the blade is of 6A steel, with a hardness of 57-59 Rc. The blade of this model has a double concave back edge, which gives it a distinctive profile similar to that of the SOG Tech knives.

The handle is full and contoured, with shallow finger grooves. It is made of black micarta, with lines that flow smoothly into the contoured brass double guard and butt. Coloured spacers add to the distinctly up-market appearance, which despite its good looks is an immensely practical blade, highly effective as a fighter and good for general field and camp tasks as well. As with any clip point design, however, this blade is not well suited to digging or prying.

Al Mar also make a larger knife under the SF-Sog Special Ops name, with a 'B' suffix to the product code. This measures 12in. overall, with an 8in. blade of the Randall Mk I style. The micarta handle is of a more utilitarian design, with deeper finger grooves and a plainer stainless steel guard. Although not so pretty to look at as its namesake, it is a fearsome fighting weapon and practical field tool.

Manufacturer:	Al Mar Knives Inc., Lake Oswego, Oregon, USA
Model:	SF-Sog Special Ops (A1 model)
Length overall:	11 3/4in. ('B' model 13in.)
Blade length:	6 5/8in. (('B' model 8in.)
Blade shape:	Clip point
Blade material:	6A steel, Rc 57-59
Edge:	Hollow ground with false top edge
Grip:	Black micarta; brass guard and butt; lanyard hole
Construction:	Full-length tang
Sheath:	Black leather belt sheath

Alan Wood is a custom knifemaker based in Cumbria, England, who makes a range of well-regarded hunting knives as well as a small selection of military patterns. His Model 14 'Serviceman' is a full-sized combat knife on the Randall theme, with a straight clip point 7in. blade. Wood describes this knife as 'primarily a heavy duty field tool, but one that will cope with use as a last ditch weapon'. The handle is contoured, and the lines flow continuously into the contoured double guard and butt.

A shorter 'Pilot' version of this knife is also available, with a 5 1/2in. blade. This also has a flatter handle so it may be carried less obtrusively.

Being a custom knife, the Model 14 is available in a number of variations to the customer's order. The handle, for instance, may be of micarta, exotic hardwood or other material, and a sub-hilt may be added. Guard and butt may be brass, nickel silver, bronze, blued steel or stainless steel, and engraving can be arranged to order. Blade finish may be satin, mirror polish or matt beadblasted.

Wood also makes other knives intended for military use, including an 8 1/4in. concealment boot knife, an 11in. dirk, and a 10 1/4in. modern fighter named the 'Sentinel'.

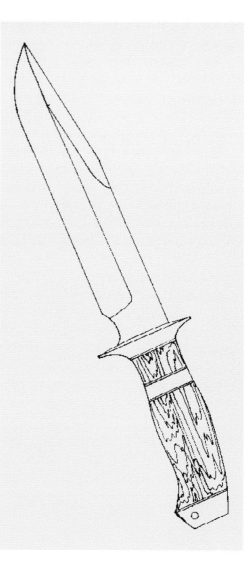

Manufacturer:	Alan Wood, Carlisle, Cumbria, England
Model:	Mod 14 Serviceman
Length overall:	11 3/4in.
Blade length:	7in.
Blade shape:	Bowie
Blade material:	Steel
Edge:	Hollow-ground
Grip:	One-piece hardwood handle with lanyard hole
Construction:	Full-length narrow radiused tang with buttcap; guard pinned and soldered
Sheath:	Handmade knife. Choice of sheaths possible

Blackjack's AWAC is a knife designed to withstand the most extreme conditions, hence the name AWAC: All Weather, All Conditions. It is a medium-sized knife, measuring 10 1/2in. overall with a 6in. blade. The materials used in its construction are chosen to live up to the name - 440A stainless steel for the blade and furniture, and black micarta for the handle.

Unusually for a military knife, the blade is flat ground, and has a drop point shape. The blade follows the line of the ricasso, with a small choil separating the two. This type of blade is good for food preparation and similar jobs involving slicing and skinning, but is less well suited to heavy chopping, prying and similar jobs. It is also not the blade of choice for fighting, although a good deal better than nothing in a tight spot.

The AWAC's handle is contoured, with a straight back and a finger groove. It is flared towards the butt, giving a firm hold. There is a lanyard hole, formed from a stainless steel tube which pins the handle to the tang, and the knife comes in a black leather belt sheath.

Manufacturer:	Blackjack Knives, Effingham, Illinois, USA
Model:	AWAC
Length overall:	10 1/2in.
Blade length:	6in.
Blade shape:	Drop point
Blade material:	440A stainless steel, satin finish
Edge:	Flat-grind
Grip:	Black micarta with finger groove for index finger, and lanyard hole
Construction:	Full-length tang
Sheath:	Black leather belt sheath

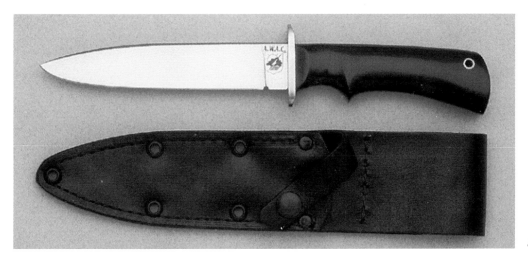

The acronym HALO stands for High Altitude Low Opening - a parachuting tactic used by special forces for covert insertion into enemy-held territory. The use of this term as a name for this Blackjack knife clearly implies that it is intended for special forces use and its general design would appear to confirm this.

The Blackjack HALO is a solidly built, medium-sized combat knife, measuring 10in. overall, with an extended clip blade in the Randall style.

The handle is a solid, rectangular section, slab of micarta, with four deep finger grooves and a thick, straight brass double guard. The knife comes with a lined black Cordura belt sheath with leg tie.

This is a hefty general purpose combat knife, well suited to most field chores, and which would prove effective as a fighter when needed.

Manufacturer:	Blackjack Knives, Effingham, Illinois, USA
Model:	HALO
Length overall:	10in.
Blade length:	5 1/2in.
Blade shape:	Clip-point with extended false back edge
Blade material:	Carbon steel, satin finish
Edge:	Bevel-grind
Grip:	Black micarta with four pronounced finger grooves, and lanyard hole
Construction:	Brass double hilt
Sheath:	Black Cordura belt sheath with leg tie

Blackjack Knives produce a number of knives in their 1-7 series, all of which are modern copies of the famous Randall Model 1 combat knife.

The story goes that Walter Doane 'Bo' Randall began making knives in 1937, when he could not find another knife like one he had seen made by Bill Scagle. What began as a hobby became a flourishing business after Captain Zacharias of the US Navy asked Randall to make him a fighting knife, shortly before the USA entered the Second World War. The design became known as the Model 1, or 'All Purpose Fighting Knife'. As Randall's reputation spread, he received orders from US servicemen all over the world - including Captain Ronald Reagan of the USAAF.

Later designs included the Model 2 'Fighting Stiletto', inspired by the Fairbairn-Sykes Fighting Knife, the Bowie bladed Model 14 'Attack', and a hollow-handled sawback survival knife, the Model 18 'Attack Survival'.

Randall's Model 1 was offered with a 6in., 7in. or 8in. blade of 1/4in. stock, in a choice of carbon steel or stainless. Blackjack's modern reproductions are carbon steel, with a 7in. blade.

Randall's original knives had stacked leather washer or micarta handles. The current Blackjack models offer these options as well as staghorn. As with the originals, the Blackjack 1-7 may be obtained with or without a steel butt; decorative spacers are used between the handle itself and the guard and/or butt. One model, the Subhilt, has a single guard 1 1/8in. back from the double guard. This acts as a finger groove and provides extra grip.

The Randall Model 1 and its modern copies is one of the most highly prized fighting/combat knife designs among US and other servicemen around the world, which have seen extensive use in conflicts since the Second World War.

Manufacturer:	Blackjack Knives, Effingham, Illinois, USA
Model:	Classic Model 1-7
Length overall:	12in.
Blade length:	7in.
Blade shape:	Randall-style Bowie
Blade material:	Carbon steel
Edge:	Bevel-grind
Grip:	Stacked leather washer (micarta or staghorn also available)
Construction:	Handle on full-length tang with brass double guard and duralumin butt
Sheath:	Leather belt sheath

The Buck Master is perhaps the most widely known of the combat/survival knife type, encompassing popular features such as a hollow handle and sawback in a big, hefty knife. Measuring a little over 12in. overall, the Buck Master is based on the M9 bayonet design. It is a Bowie-style knife, with a 7 1/2in. clip point blade, a wide double guard, and a grooved and chequered steel tube handle with screw-on butt cap.

The blade has a plain convex main edge and a heavily serrated clip edge. On the spine of the blade is a saw-toothed edge, with rear-facing teeth. It is a versatile blade which, although not really suited to heavy chopping, will tackle most jobs required of a big knife in the field, and may also be used for fighting if necessary. The serrated clip edge can be useful for tough materials like hide and webbing, but the saw edge is much less effective than a purpose-made saw for cutting wood, bone and the like - the teeth hang up in the work and clog quickly. The saw teeth are also a distinct disadvantage if the knife is used as a fighter, as they tend to hang-up in the opponent's body, making withdrawal difficult.

The handle's grooved and chequered surface gives good grip, although being plain steel it is cold to the touch and may freeze to a bare hand in sub-zero conditions. It is also not very forgiving when the knife is used for heavy work, transmitting all the shock of heavy chopping strokes to the hand, wrist and arm. Some users wrap the handle of this knife in paracord, which not only makes the grip more comfortable but also provides a handy length of cord for emergency use.

The butt is a screw-on cap, under which is a hollow where are stored the two anchor pins. These screw into threaded holes in the guard, allowing the knife to be used as an anchor or grapple, with a line attached to the lanyard point at the butt. While this could conceivably be a useful feature in certain circumstances, users should bear in mind the consequences if the knife breaks free from its hold while there is tension on the line. A conventional grapple coming towards you at speed is bad enough, but one with a 7 1/2in. blade is doubly unpleasant.

There is sufficient space in the hollow handle to store

small survival items along with the anchor pins. If the anchor pins are discarded, of course, one may then carry considerably more survival gear.

The sheath and its accessories are an important part of the Buck Master system. The sheath is similar to that for the M9 bayonet, although it lacks the wire-cutter attachment. The sheath itself is made of rigid plastic, with a nylon webbing belt hanger and attachment slots for a webbing pouch which may be used to store small items, including a Silva compass which is available as an accessory. The sheath also incorporates a sharpening stone and has a cord leg tie.

This knife has proved popular with the civilian market and with some soldiers. My personal opinion is that the compromises necessary to provide this number of features in a knife reduce its usefulness for general tasks, and I would choose to carry a knife with a more conventional and simpler design.

Manufacturer: Buck Knives, El Cajon, California, USA

Model: Buck Master

Length overall: 12 1/2in.

Blade length: 7 1/2in.

Blade shape: Bowie

Blade material: Stainless steel. Satin or parkerised finish available

Edge: Hollow-grind main edge; serrated clip edge; saw back

Grip: Steel tube with grooves and chequering

Construction: Hollow steel tube handle with screw-on butt cap; double guard

Features: Anchor pins - stowed in handle - screw into threaded holes in guard for use as grapple. Lanyard attachment ring under pommel.

Sheath: Plastic and Cordura sheath includes sharpening stone and attachment points for accessory pouch

The Nighthawk is a relatively recent addition to Buck's range, and one that has quickly found favour with military users. It is a medium-sized combat/field knife, with a sharply pointed 6 1/4in. straight clip blade shaped a little like the Randall Model 1. The blade is well suited for stabbing, piercing and cutting, but lacks heft and forward weight for chopping. The tip is fine enough for quite delicate work, but is not really strong enough to be used for prying. The blade has a barely discernible reverse curve, which gives it a little more cutting power.

The handle of this knife is unusual in design and proves to be very effective. It is formed of a skeleton made of hard, black, Kevlar-reinforced Zytel, with infills of soft Alcryn with a textured and pimpled surface. One large Alcryn insert forms the contoured belly of the handle, while another smaller insert is placed on top of the handle just behind the guard, where the thumb falls. The textured surface and contoured shape of the handle by themselves would give excellent grip, but added to this is the softness of the Alcryn, which yields slightly to the pressure of the hand, essentially moulding itself to the contours of the fingers. The soft handle material has another useful feature - it helps to absorb the impact of a chopping stroke, dulling any vibrations that are set up in the knife rather than transferring them to the bones of the hand and wrist. This allows the knife to be used for extended heavy tasks with comfort.

It is worth noting that, despite its contoured shape, the handle lends itself to alternative holds. It sits well in the fencing hold advocated by Fairbairn and Sykes (see entry for the Fairbairn Sykes Fighting Knife) and may also be reversed in the hand for a downward stab to the carotid or subclavian artery. The shape of the handle means that one remains aware of the knife's orientation in the hand - unlike a simple round handle which does not transmit this sense. The grip can be choked up for fine work, although the short ricasso and lack of choil mean that the first finger must remain hooked around the lower guard to avoid its being cut on the edge of the blade.

The Nighthawk comes with a well-fitted Cordura sheath, with a plastic insert for stiffness. It holds the blade well, keeping it firmly in place even if turned upside down and shaken, and there is a press-studded retention loop for added security.

Manufacturer:	Buck Knives, El Cajon, California, USA
Model:	Nighthawk
Length overall:	11 1/4in.
Blade length:	6 1/4in.
Blade shape:	Sharply-pointed clip point design with false back edge
Blade material:	425 steel with black oxide finish
Edge:	Hollow-grind
Grip:	Kevlar reinforced Zytel ST-801, with contoured dimpled Alcryn inserts and thumb rest
Construction:	Handle moulded on to tang
Sheath:	Black Cordura belt sheath

Now being partially replaced by Eickhorn's ACK, this knife has for many years been the issue combat knife of the German *Bundeswehr*. Measuring 10 3/8in. overall, it has a relatively plain looking 5 11/16in. drop point blade of 420 stainless steel. The guard is made of steel and is extended at the bottom for extra protection of the hand. The grip is made of green plastic scales, which are held on the tang by screws, the rear one of which incorporates a lanyard hole. The handle is contoured, with a central bulge, and flares out again at grip and butt. The scabbard is made of steel, with a leather frog for attachment to the soldier's belt.

Manufacturer:	Distributed by United Cutlery, Sevierville, Tennessee, USA
Model:	UC855 Bundeswehr Knife
Length overall:	10 3/8in.
Blade length:	5 11/16in.
Blade shape:	Drop point
Blade material:	1/8in. thick 420 stainless steel
Edge:	Bevel-ground
Grip:	Green impact-resistant plastic with lanyard hole; steel crossguard
Construction:	Grip pinned to full-length tang with threaded screws
Sheath:	Metal scabbard with leather frog

The 1219C2 USMC Fighting/Utility knife has become the definitive American combat knife. It was first issued to US troops during World War II, and early models were manufactured by Union Cutlery under the Ka-Bar trademark. Consequently the design became universally known as the 'Kabar', although over the years the knife has been made by several US companies, including Case and Ontario, to Department of Defense specifications.

Camillus Cutlery Co. produced the first knives of this pattern in 1942, and their version of the 'Kabar' has long been widely respected by US soldiers. During the Vietnam War, it was issued to many personnel and was a popular private purchase for those who were not issued with it. In Vietnam and other conflicts, servicemen used the Kabar for all manner of field chores, from shelter building to preparing food, and it was widely recognised as a versatile and reliable tool.

The knife is utilitarian in looks and design. It consists of a 7in. Bowie type clip point blade, with a fuller or 'blood grove' on both sides. The clip edge is slightly concave and is sharpened. The blade is made of carbon steel, with a Parkerised protective finish. There is a straight double guard made of steel, and the handle is made of leather washers stacked on the tang and held in place with a steel butt cap pinned through the end of the tang. This cap may be used as a light hammer for tent pegs and the like.

The grooved leather handle gives a good grip, although being of a natural material it will eventually degrade in jungle conditions, despite the preservatives added by the manufacturers.

The knife comes with a black leather welted, stitched and riveted sheath, with belt loop, press studded retention loop, and a hole at the tip for a leg tie.

The Marine Combat is a compromise design, as any combat knife must be. The blade is a little light for chopping, and does not have the strength needed for heavy prying, but its relative thinness (0.16in.) helps it to cut better than a thick blade. It also keeps the knife's total weight down - an important factor for a soldier who must carry his equipment on his body. Kabars have been known to break when used for prying and throwing, but

there are many reports of their effectiveness in combat. Here again, the design's compromises show up: it is not an ideal shape either for stabbing or for hacking/slashing, but combat experience has proved that it is more than capable.

An almost identical knife is available, with a brown leather grip, in a tan leather sheath stamped with the USMC initials and the globe, anchor and eagle device of the US Marine Corps

Manufacturer:	Camillus Cutlery Co., Camillus, New York, USA
Model:	Marine Combat
Length overall:	12in.
Blade length:	7in.
Blade shape:	Bowie with fuller
Blade material:	Carbon steel with protective black phosphate finish
Edge:	Bevel-ground, with sharpened clip edge
Grip:	Black leather, grooved
Construction:	Stacked leather washers on full-length tang, with steel butt-cap
Sheath:	Black leather welted sheath

The Mk 3 Trench Knife is a simple utility/fighting design, based on the M4 bayonet, but without attachments to fit it to a rifle. The blade is a parallel-sided spear point, measuring 6 3/4in. long. It has one sharp edge and a false back edge. Construction is similar to that of other US military knives, such as the Marine Combat, with a simple oval steel guard and leather washers stacked on a narrow tang and finished off with a steel butt cap pinned through the end of the tang.

This is a good, dependable utility/fighter, with the added advantage that its relatively cheap construction makes it dispensable and consequently, easily replaced. It is rather too light for heavy duty chopping and prying but is otherwise reliable for general jobs.

Manufacturer:	Camillus Cutlery Co., Camillus, New York, USA
Model:	Mk 3 Trench Knife
Length overall:	11 5/8in.
Blade length:	6 3/4in.
Blade shape:	Spear point
Blade material:	Carbon steel with black phosphate finish
Edge:	Bevel-grind with false back edge
Grip:	Brown leather, grooved
Construction:	Stacked leather washers on full-length tang
Sheath:	Brown leather belt sheath with leg tie

Similar in construction to that of the well-known Kabar, the USAF Pilot Survival Knife is carried by aircrew and other personnel for survival use in the event of an aircraft being forced to land in inhospitable or enemy-held territory. The knife is shorter than the Kabar types, at 9 1/2in. overall, with a 5 1/8in. blade. The blade is slightly bellied, with a concave clip edge, and has a saw-tooth back. It is coated with a protective black phosphate finish. The handle is formed from stacked brown leather washers and topped off with a hexagonal pommel which may be used for hammering.

This knife is smaller and lighter than the standard Kabar types, making it easier for aircrew to carry on their clothing without its getting in the way. However, it is a strong and versatile knife which has proved invaluable, both for survival tasks like shelter building and as a last-ditch fighting weapon. It should be noted, however, that any saw back may hang-up in an opponent's body and be difficult to withdraw, with potentially disastrous consequences.

The Camillus version comes with a light tan leather belt sheath, with a pouch for a sharpening stone. Many service personnel dispose of the stone, and replace it with a small Swiss Army type knife for delicate tasks, creating a highly versatile package which occupies little space and weight.

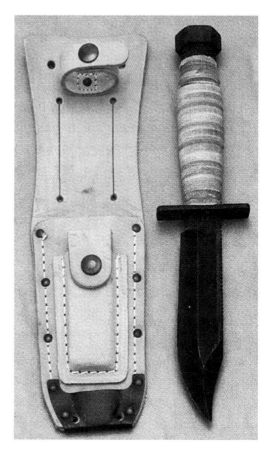

Manufacturer:	Camillus Cutlery Co., Camillus, New York, USA
Model:	Pilot Survival Knife
Length overall:	9 1/2in.
Blade length:	5 1/8in.
Blade shape:	Bowie with saw back
Blade material:	Carbon steel with protective black phosphate finish
Edge:	Bevel-ground, with false clip edge and saw-tooth back edge
Grip:	Brown leather, grooved, with hexagonal steel pommel
Construction:	Stacked leather washers on full-length tang
Sheath:	Brown leather sheath with sharpening stone in pouch

The Chris Reeve Aviator is based firmly on the USAF-issue Pilot Survival knife, and at first glance closely resembles it in size and blade shape. Indeed, the Aviator is made for the same purpose, but any similarity ends there. Chris Reeve knives are made from a single piece of steel, a design trait which completely side-steps any problems of strength at the join of tang and blade; the handle and blade are one continuous piece of steel. Like all Chris Reeve knives, the Aviator is also finished to a much higher standard than is possible in a mass-produced, military-issue knife.

The Aviator is made from A2 steel, measures 8in. overall and weighs 5 1/2oz. The 4in. blade is a Bowie style, with a straight false edge clip, and there is a saw-toothed edge on the spine. This saw is said by Reeve to be designed for versatility rather than excellence in any one task - 'it can be used to saw most material, although none perfectly'.

The handle is tubular and has a chequered surface for extra grip. A narrow section near the guard allows the knife to be grasped firmly by the thumb and first finger. The handle is hollow and capped by a hexagonal, screw-on pommel with a lanyard hole. The pommel is designed to screw up to the shoulder of the threaded section, so that it may be used for hammering without damaging the threads. A neoprene O-ring seals the recess inside, which may be used to store matches and other small survival items.

The Aviator, like other Chris Reeve designs, is highly regarded, and a popular private purchase item with military personnel. Users report that one of its few drawbacks is the grip, which being bare steel is cold to the touch in low temperatures and may turn in the hand owing to its round cross-section.

The knife comes with a pancake-style leather sheath with belt slots.

Manufacturer:	Chris Reeve, Boise, Idaho, USA
Model:	Aviator
Length overall:	8in.
Blade length:	4in.
Blade shape:	Clip point with saw back
Blade material:	A2 steel, Kal-Gard coated
Edge:	Bevel-ground with false clip edge, and saw-tooth back
Grip:	One-piece chequered, tubular section steel, with lanyard hole in hexagonal pommel
Construction:	Ground from single piece of steel; hollow handle with screw-on pommel
Sheath:	Flat 'pancake' leather sheath with twin slits for webbing or belt

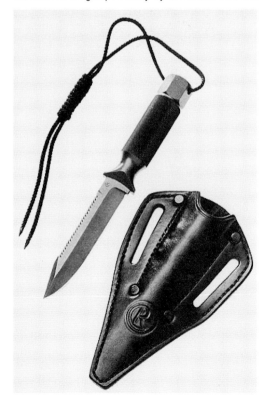

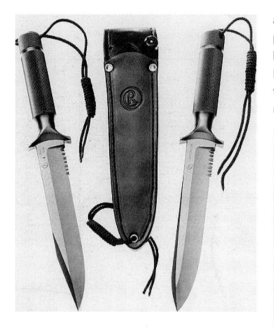

a nylon stud for retention, which holds the knife firmly in place even when it is worn inverted on webbing, but can be pushed out of engagement with the thumb as the knife is withdrawn. The stud can be fitted on the right or the left of the sheath for the correspondingly handed user.

Manufacturer:	Chris Reeve, Boise, Idaho, USA
Model:	Project I
Length overall:	12 3/4in.
Blade length:	7 1/2in.
Blade shape:	Spear point with serrated section near hilt (Project II has clip point blade shape)
Blade material:	A2 steel, Kal-Gard coated
Edge:	Bevel-ground
Grip:	One-piece chequered, tubular section steel, with lanyard hole in matching pommel
Construction:	Ground from single piece of steel; hollow handle with screw-on pommel
Sheath:	Leather sheath with leg tie and nylon retaining stud

The Chris Reeve Project I and II were designed in conjunction with Sgt Karl Lippard, who served with the USMC and wrote *The Warrior*. Like the Aviator, they are one-piece designs, made from a single piece of A2 steel. This makes them immensely strong, while leaving a hollow handle which may be used for the storage of small survival items (see the Aviator, for a description of the general construction).

The Project I and II were designed to fulfil all the functions that Sgt Lippard felt were vital for a knife carried by a Marine. The 7 1/2in. blade will chop, dig and cut, and has sufficient 'meat' up front for maximum strength and good balance. The wave serrations on the main edge are shaped to cut easily through nylon cord or webbing. The 2in. cross guard has a night index which tells the user by touch which way up the knife is in the hand.

The Project I has an immensely strong spear point blade, which gives a particularly strong tip for digging and prying. The Project II has a more traditionally styled clip point blade, giving a finer point which is still more than strong enough for most jobs. Both knives are 12 3/4in. long overall, have 7 1/2in. blades, and weigh 14oz.

The Project knives come with a stitched and riveted black leather sheath with belt loop and leg tie. There is

The Shadow III and IV are two more in Chris Reeve's one-piece knife range; see the descriptions of his Aviator and Project knives for details of their general construction. The Shadow III is 8in. overall, with a 4in. spear point blade, and weighs 6oz. The Shadow IV is larger at 10 1/2in. overall, weighing 11 1/2oz with a 5 1/2in. blade. Both knives have double guard and are noted for the strength of the spear point tip. Reeve says that this design 'has been used by professional soldiers all over the world, who have found them to be extremely good weapons as well as rugged dependable tools.'

Manufacturer:	Chris Reeve, Boise, Idaho, USA
Model:	Shadow IV
Length overall:	10 1/2in. (Shadow III 8in.)
Blade length:	5 1/2in. (Shadow III 4in.)
Blade shape:	Spear point
Blade material:	A2 steel, Kal-Gard coated
Edge:	Bevel-ground, with false back edge
Grip:	One-piece chequered, tubular section steel, with lanyard hole in matching pommel
Construction:	Ground from single piece of steel; hollow handle with screw-on pommel
Sheath:	Slim symmetrical sheath with snap loop over crossguard and snap fastener on belt loop. (Shadow III has flat 'pancake' leather sheath with twin slits for webbing or belt)

Cold Steel's Black Bear Classic is a sub-hilt design first developed by Bob Loveless. It is primarily intended as a fighter, with an 8in. blade that gives good reach and excellent penetration. The sub-hilt gives a very firm hold, and aids withdrawal of the knife from an opponent's body, although restricting the use of alternative holds.

The blade is almost a dagger shape, with a diamond-shaped cross-section, but with a vestigial clip point. The knife is available with the back edge sharpened or unsharpened. It is made from the same high carbon stainless steel that is used in Cold Steel's Tanto series.

The handle is formed from micarta scales, which are pinned to the full tang, and the whole knife is buffed to a lustrous shine.

This is an impressive looking fighting knife but it is versatile enough to be used for a variety of jobs in the field.

Manufacturer:	Cold Steel Inc., Ventura, California, USA
Model:	Black Bear Classic
Length overall:	13 1/2in.
Blade length:	8 1/4in.
Blade shape:	Double-edged, close to dagger style, but with slight clip point (unsharpened back edge model available)
Blade material:	3/16in. thick, high carbon stainless steel
Edge:	Double edged, hollow-ground
Grip:	Black micarta handle with stainless guard and single guard subhilt; lanyard hole
Construction:	Micarta scales pinned to full tang
Sheath:	Black leather belt sheath with sharpening stone in pouch

The Bush Ranger was designed by Lynn C Thompson to fulfil the need for a rugged but light sheath knife that was large enough to be useful in a real emergency, but light enough to be worn on the belt every day in the field. Its performance belies its light weight of 8.8oz, and size of 12 1/2in. overall.

The blade is Bowie shaped, and is flat ground for maximum cutting performance. The main edge is curved continuously from the choil to the tip, giving a highly efficient draw cut. There is extra belly at the tip which is a bonus for field dressing and the skinning of game. The concave clip gives a sharp tip for piercing, which is nonetheless remarkably strong and resistant to breaking or bending.

The handle has a deep belly which fills the hand well, and its chequered Kraton rubber surface gives excellent grip, even in wet conditions.

The Bush Ranger comes with a black Cordura nylon sheath with a leg tie and double retaining straps. The knife is available with a black epoxy powder coated Carbon V steel blade, or a bright AUS 8A stainless steel version.

Manufacturer:	Cold Steel Inc., Ventura, California, USA
Model:	Bush Ranger
Length overall:	12 1/2in.
Blade length:	7 1/2in.
Blade shape:	Deep-bladed Bowie style
Blade material:	Available in AUS 8A stainless steel or black epoxy coated Carbon V steel
Edge:	Flat-ground with false clip edge
Grip:	One-piece black Kraton rubber handle in deep bellied shape, incorporating double guard and lanyard hole
Construction:	Kraton handle moulded to full-length tang
Sheath:	Black Cordura belt sheath

Cold Steel's R1 Military Classic is a modern copy of the Randall Model 1; see Blackjack Model 1-7 for details of this classic military knife.

Cold Steel make their model R1 from the same stainless steel used in their famous Tanto series. The double guard is fashioned from 300 series stainless steel, and the handle is black linen micarta with coloured fibre spacers.

The knife comes with a brown leather belt sheath, a long press-studded retaining strap and a pocket for a sharpening stone.

Manufacturer:	Cold Steel Inc., Ventura, California, USA
Model:	R1 Military Classic
Length overall:	11 7/8in.
Blade length:	7in.
Blade shape:	Randall-style straight-clip Bowie
Blade material:	3/16in. thick 400 series stainless steel
Edge:	Bevel-ground
Grip:	Contoured black linen micarta handle
Construction:	Handle fitted to full-length tang, with stainless double guard and coloured fibre spacers
Sheath:	Brown leather belt sheath with sharpening stone in pouch

The Cold Steel Recon Scout is essentially a scaled-down version of the company's Trail Master Bowie. Measuring 12 1/2in. overall, it has a 7 1/2in. Bowie-style clip point blade which is flat ground. The back edge is false ground and slightly concave. The blade is made from Carbon V steel, and has a baked-on black epoxy finish which resists corrosion and minimises reflections.

There is a straight double guard, and the handle is made of Kraton rubber, chequered for extra grip, with a brass-lined lanyard hole.

Cold Steel describe the Recon Scout as 'the strongest, toughest 7 1/2in. combat knife in the world' - not a claim that a company with their reputation would make lightly. Certainly the 'torture tests' shown in their catalogue photographs would appear to bear this out.

Manufacturer:	Cold Steel Inc., Ventura, California, USA
Model:	Recon Scout
Length overall:	12 1/2in.
Blade length:	7 1/2in.
Blade shape:	Clip point
Blade material:	5/16in. thick Carbon V steel, black epoxy powder coated
Edge:	Flat-ground with false back edge
Grip:	One-piece chequered black Kraton rubber with lanyard hole
Construction:	Kraton handle moulded to full-length tang
Sheath:	Black Cordura belt sheath

The Cold Steel SRK was designed by Lynn C Thompson as a versatile knife for survival/rescue operations - a knife that would be able to withstand extreme abuse. The blade is made of 3/16in. thick Carbon V steel, finished with black epoxy powder coating. It measures 6in. long, and has a Bowie-style clip point blade, bevel-ground in a sweeping curve for good cutting performance. The clip shape gives a fine point for good penetration and detailed work, while the blade is also heavy enough for light chopping.

The handle is Kraton rubber, with a contoured shape and integral single guard. This allows the grip to be 'choked up' for fine work. The soft, chequered surface gives a good grip in virtually any conditions and helps to absorb the shocks of use rather than transmit them to the bones of the hand and wrist.

The knife comes with a black Cordura belt sheath with a leg tie.

Manufacturer:	Cold Steel Inc., Ventura, California, USA
Model:	SRK
Length overall:	10 5/8in.
Blade length:	6in.
Blade shape:	Clip point
Blade material:	Carbon V steel, black epoxy powder coated
Edge:	Bevel-ground with false back edge
Grip:	One-piece chequered black Kraton rubber with lanyard hole
Construction:	Kraton handle moulded to full-length tang
Sheath:	Black Cordura belt sheath

Cold Steel's Trailmaster Bowie is a large, high performance knife designed by Lynn C Thompson. It measures 14 1/2in. overall and weighs just over 1lb, with a 9 1/2in. Bowie blade of 5/16in. thick Carbon V steel. The blade is hardened and tempered to give exceptional strength and flexibility. The false clip edge is slightly concave, with extra thickness near the tip, making it extremely resistant to breaking or bending. The blade is flat-ground for good cutting and slicing performance, and honed to a very sharp edge. The balance of the knife is approximately 3/4in. in front of the guard, which gives a blade-heavy feel that increases the power of chopping and slashing strokes.

The handle is 5in. long and made of chequered Kraton rubber, which gives it a non-slip, shock-absorbing grip. The cross section is contoured to help in preventing the knife turning in the hand. The double guard is relatively short so that it does not tend to become snagged in clothing or equipment.

The Trailmaster is a big, powerful knife with quite astonishing chopping and slashing performance - a photo-sequence in Cold Steel's catalogue shows Thompson chopping clean through a rope as thick as his arm with a single stroke. The knife is also extremely robust, yet remains capable of quite delicate work. It makes a highly versatile, heavy-duty field knife, which also has awesome capabilities as a fighter.

Manufacturer:	Cold Steel Inc., Ventura, California, USA
Model:	Trailmaster Bowie
Length overall:	14 1/2in.
Blade length:	9 1/2in.
Blade shape:	Bowie
Blade material:	5/16in. thick triple tempered carbon V steel
Edge:	Flat-ground with false clip edge
Grip:	One-piece chequered black Kraton rubber with lanyard hole
Construction:	Kraton handle moulded to full-length tang
Sheath:	Black Cordura belt sheath with leg tie

The Collins/Parry Knife was the result of collaboration between Steve Collins, a designer and martial artist, and Mel Parry, who served with British special forces. Their aim was to produce the definitive combat survival knife - a true working tool. The knife is fairly simple at first glance, with a bellied Bolo-type clipped blade. But on closer inspection it offers several different cutting edges and holds, making it extremely versatile.

The knife is strong and heavy, with the blade made from 1/4in. thick high tensile carbon spring steel hardened to 57-58 Rc. The main edge is bevel-ground for strength. The deep belly shape takes the weight forward, giving the knife a powerful chopping stroke. The point looks clipped in shape but is ground as a spear point, which is strong enough for digging and prying. Near the choil is a hollow-ground section which can be honed to razor sharpness for fine cutting and whittling jobs such as making fire sticks. On the spine of the blade is a serrated edge which may be used for sawing through rope, webbing or gristle.

The knife is of full-tang construction, with micarta scales screwed to the tang. These are contoured with a deep belly and chequered for extra grip. The steel double guard is also contoured, with its lines flowing continuously into the scales, to be kinder on the hand. It is designed with relatively short guards so that one can choke up the grip for fine work - the ricasso is extended and has finger grooves which make the choke grip firm and comfortable.

The steel butt is squared off on two sides so that it may be used as a hammer in either direction. The flats are file-cut to reduce any tendency for them to skid off the work on striking. The butt also incorporates a lanyard hole.

A variation on the original design has the blade angled downwards, in the manner of a kukri.

I first handled this knife at the COPEX show in 1995 and was immediately impressed with its heft and handling. It is a true working tool, designed by people who use knives professionally and know what is needed in a combat survival knife. I was told that the knife had been selected for Richard Branson's attempt at a round-the-world balloon flight, and that several special forces

units had shown interest. At the time of writing, however, the knife has not gone into production and only a few pre-production models exist. With the current British political climate, it is doubtful whether the Collins/Parry Knife will ever become widely available, which would be a loss to military and civilians alike.

Manufacturer:	Portfolio Section V, Stockport, Cheshire, UK
Model:	Collins/Parry Knife
Length overall:	13 3/4in.
Blade length:	8 3/4in.
Blade shape:	Bolo/Bowie-type with serrated back edge
Blade material:	1/4in. thick high tensile carbon spring steel EN9
Edge:	Main edge bevel-ground; hollow ground section near choil for extra sharpness
Grip:	Chequered and contoured micarta scales. Contoured double guard and butt, the butt squared off and file-cut for use as hammer
Construction:	Scales screwed to full tang
Sheath:	Leather belt sheath with leg tie

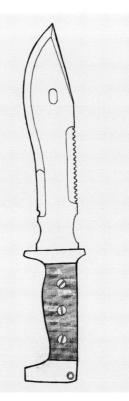

Developed for the German *Bundeswehr* in the late 1980s, Eickhorn's ACK is a modern, multi-function combat knife with many advanced features. As well as the *Bundeswehr*, it has since been adopted by a number of other military forces around the world.

The knife is basically a Bowie-type combat knife with a moulded plastic handle. It is remarkably light, at around 220g, or a total of 430g with sheath. The blade is carbon steel, with a black chemical finish, and has a bevel-ground main edge and concave false clip edge. The spine has a sophisticated saw edge, with teeth set alternately left and right to remove material to the thickness of the blade; this avoids the blade's jamming as it saws through wood, bone or the like.

The moulded plastic handle is contoured and grooved for grip and incorporates a double guard. The handle is flattened at the sides, giving the knife a thinner profile so that it rides less obtrusively on the belt. Set into the top guard is a steel extension which may be used as a bottle opener and has a notch for wire stripping. The handle has a hollow compartment which can store small survival items.

The scabbard has a quick-release clip so that it may be removed from the belt and used in conjunction with the knife to form a scissor-action wire cutter. There is also a screwdriver at the tip of the scabbard.

The knife is electrically insulated and resistant to fungal and NBC agents. It is tested to between -40 and +80°C, and may be decontaminated.

Manufacturer:	Eickhorn GmbH, Solingen, Germany
Model:	ACK (Advanced Combat Knife)
Length overall:	11 11/16in.
Blade length:	6 5/8in.
Blade shape:	Bowie-type clip point
Blade material:	Carbon steel with black chemical finish
Edge:	Bevel-ground
Grip:	Moulded contoured, glass-reinforced plastic with grooves, incorporating double guard
Construction:	Plastic grip moulded on to tang
Sheath:	Rigid plastic sheath incorporating wire-cutter attachment and sharpening stone, with detachable hanger with clip for military web belt

The Eickhorn KCB 77 CS is identical to the company's KCB 77 bayonet, except that it does not have the fittings for attachment to an assault rifle. Refer to the relevant entry earlier for details.

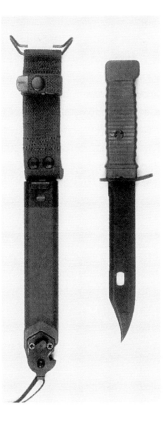

Manufacturer: Eickhorn GmbH, Solingen, Germany

Model: ACK (Advanced Combat Knife)

Length overall: 11 11/16in.

Blade length: 6 5/8in.

Blade shape: Clip point

Blade material: Carbon steel with corrosion-resistant black finish

Edge: Bevel-ground

Grip: Ribbed and contoured plastic scales, rectangular section

Construction: Scales fitted to full-length tang

Sheath: Sophisticated rigid plastic sheath with wire cutter, screwdriver tip, and clip attachment to belt hanger

Carried by the Swedish National Defence forces, the F1 is a small utility knife with a Kraton handle and a 3 3/4in. drop point, flat ground blade. It comes in a flapped leather belt sheath.

This knife is handy for light work, but would be of little use for fighting, or for chopping or slashing. It is no bigger than many pocket folders, but offers more strength and rigidity due to its non-folding design. It is a good quality item, made from modern materials which offer high performance and resistance to corrosion.

Manufacturer:	Solingen, Germany
Model:	F1
Length overall:	8 1/4in.
Blade length:	3 3/4in.
Blade shape:	Drop point
Blade material:	ATS 34 stainless steel
Edge:	Flat-ground
Grip:	Black chequered Kraton rubber grip with lanyard hole
Construction:	Kraton grip moulded on to tang
Sheath:	Full black leather pistol flap style sheath

Gerber's BMF is a big, solid knife well capable of the heaviest chopping, hacking and slashing. Designed as 'the ultimate survival knife system', it makes a versatile field tool, as well as an effective close-combat weapon. The initials BMF stand for Basic Multi-Function, although the troops often refer to it as the 'Big Mother F***er'.

The knife is a massive 14in. overall, with a heavy 9in. Bowie-type blade with a long, straight, false edge clip. The blade is 1/4in. thick high carbon stainless steel, with a bevel-ground edge. The blade comes to a fine point at the tip, offering good penetration. A saw back version is available, although the saw has been criticised as being relatively ineffective, jamming and clogging too easily.

The handle is Hypolon rubber, which offers a soft, comfortable grip that absorbs vibration, although its smooth surface can slip in the hand under extreme conditions. The double guard has two holes, with another hole in the single butt guard. These can be used for lashing the knife to a pole for use as a spear, or to attach a lanyard. There is a truncated cone pommel which can be used as a hammer or in combat as a 'skull crusher'.

The sheath is a strong unit of Cordura, with a belt loop and Bianchi clip. There is a pouch for a Silva compass (included with the knife), and a leg tie.

The Gerber BMF is a popular private purchase among military personnel. It is a good looking and rugged field tool which can also serve as a close-combat weapon if necessary. It is immensely practical for survival tasks such as shelter building, trap making, clearing brush and heavy undergrowth, and dressing out all sizes of game. If anything it is too big for some more delicate jobs and is best carried in conjunction with a good small knife or multi-tool.

Manufacturer:	Gerber (a division of Fiskars Inc.), Portland, Oregon, USA
Model:	BMF
Length overall:	14in.
Blade length:	9in.
Blade shape:	Bowie style clip point
Blade material:	1/4in. thick, high carbon stainless steel with satin finish
Edge:	Angle-ground, clip false edge. Saw back version available
Grip:	Hypolon rubber, contoured, with double guard and single guard at butt, truncated cone pommel
Construction:	Full- length tang
Sheath:	Black Cordura lined belt sheath with leg tie, compass, and diamond sharpening stone on rear

Gerber's Bowie is a traditionally shaped, big Bowie knife, with a 9 1/2in. flat ground blade made from 5/16in. thick, high carbon stainless steel. The knife measures 14 1/2in. overall, and weighs 18oz. The handle is a 'coffin' shape and is made of Kraton rubber moulded on to a full-length tang. It has a brass double guard and a lanyard hole. The knife comes with a Cordura sheath with belt loop and leg tie.

This is a big, well-balanced, heavy knife which is well up to heavy hacking, chopping and slashing. It would make an effective survival or field tool, as well as an effective and intimidating combat weapon.

Manufacturer:	Gerber (a division of Fiskars Inc.), Portland, Oregon, USA
Model:	Bowie
Length overall:	14 1/2in.
Blade length:	9 1/2in.
Blade shape:	Bowie clip point
Blade material:	5/16in. thick, high carbon stainless steel with satin finish
Edge:	Flat ground, clip false edge
Grip:	Coffin-shaped Kraton rubber grip with brass double guard and lanyard hole
Construction:	Handle moulded on to full-length tang
Sheath:	Black Cordura belt sheath

The Gerber LMF is a scaled-down version of the BMF. The initials stand for Light Multi-Function. The basic style and construction of the knife are the same as for the BMF. The LMF measures 10 5/8in. overall, with a 6in. blade, so it is by no means a small knife, even though it is dwarfed by its big brother.

The LMF is not simply a sized-down version of the BMF, however; there are some significant differences, especially in the handle. Here there is no butt guard, and the guard and butt are shaped so that their contours are continuous with the shape of the Hypolon rubber grip, which, unlike the BMF, also has finger grooves.

Blade shape is similar to that of the BMF, and there is the same option of a saw back. The sheath is black Cordura nylon, with a belt loop and leg strap assembly, but lacks the diamond sharpening hone which is found in the BMF sheath.

Manufacturer:	Gerber (a division of Fiskars Inc.), Portland, Oregon, USA
Model:	LMF
Length overall:	10 5/8in.
Blade length:	6in.
Blade shape:	Bowie style clip point
Blade material:	1/4in. thick, high carbon stainless steel with satin finish
Edge:	Angle-ground, clip false edge. Saw back version available
Grip:	Hypolon rubber, with two finger grooves, double guard, and matching stainless pommel
Construction:	Full-length tang
Sheath:	Black Cordura lined belt sheath with leg tie

The Gerber Patriot is a solidly made and straightforward combat survival knife, with the distinctive feature that it is intended for airborne troops - it is one of the few 'jump certified' knives for paratroopers. Designed by Blackie Collins, it has a 6in. blade and measures 10 5/8in. overall. The blade is a Bowie-style, with a long clip false edge. It is made of stainless steel with a black finish. The handle is made from moulded Zytel, with chequering and longitudinal grooves for extra grip. It is contoured to provide a finger groove for the first finger. The handle is screwed through the full-length tang and there is a cylindrical butt piece with a lanyard hole.

Perhaps the most remarkable feature of this knife is its sheath. This is made of rigid black plastic which gives a high level of protection to the blade, so that the blade will not break through and injure the user if he falls on it upon landing. There is a two-stage locking mechanism which comprises a clip and locking latch.

When the knife is slid into the sheath, the clip catches the tip of the guard and clicks into place, holding the knife securely. A violent movement could cause the knife to break free, however, so the locking latch can be moved up with the thumb into the locked position. This holds the clip so that it cannot open, ensuring that the knife remains in its sheath even if it is knocked hard in a heavy fall.

I have tried the system and found it very effective. My only reservation was that the knife rattles loudly in the sheath when it is withdrawn or replaced, making it unsuitable for close observation patrols and similar types of operation.

Manufacturer:	Gerber (a division of Fiskars Inc.), Portland, Oregon, USA
Model:	Patriot
Length overall:	10 5/8in.
Blade length:	6in.
Blade shape:	Bowie-style clip point
Blade material:	0.240in. thick, high carbon stainless steel with black oxide finish
Edge:	Angle-ground, clip false edge
Grip:	Moulded Zytel handle with chequering and lateral grooves, finger groove
Construction:	Full-length tang
Sheath:	Rigid black plastic sheath incorporates safety-catch locking device that holds knife securely in an inverted position on webbing or during violent physical activity

The kukri may seem an odd knife to include in this section; it is known and feared world-wide as the fighting weapon of the Gurkhas. However, the kukri is much more than a weapon, it is a highly effective field tool which is favoured by many experts besides the Gurkhas themselves for jungle survival use.

The kukri comes in many variations, but the one described here is fairly typical of the type issued to Gurkha soldiers in the British Army. It has a heavy, downward curved blade of thick carbon steel, measuring 7/16in. at the spine. This thins towards the sharpened edge, which is bevelled. The handle is hand-carved from buffalo horn, with a pronounced flare at the butt and is fitted to a full-length tang, with brass bolster cap and butt cap. The knife comes in a wooden block sheath which is covered with black leather. It has a brass chape and a leather frog for attachment to a belt.

The kukri's weight and blade shape provide superb chopping, hacking and slashing performance. The heavy blade chops powerfully through logs and branches, and the reverse curve edge cuts deeply with little effort. The kukri is almost unmatched for heavy survival tasks such as shelter building and clearing vegetation and can also be used for surprisingly delicate work. It also excels as a close-combat weapon, where the power of its chopping stroke is legendary - tales abound of Gurkhas lopping off the heads of their enemies with a single stroke. Some of the legend and mystique surrounding the kukri is fantasy, but there is no denying that it is a very useful jungle survival tool and a highly effective weapon.

Manufacturer:	Nepalese workshops
Model:	British Army issue type
Length overall:	15 3/4in.
Blade length:	11in.
Blade shape:	Bolo type, with pronounced downward curve
Blade material:	7/16in. max. thickness carbon steel
Edge:	Bevel
Grip:	Hand-carved buffalo horn with brass bolster and butt
Construction:	Full-length tang
Sheath:	Leather-covered wooden block sheath with leather belt frog

The Aitor Jungle King II was one of the first hollow-handled survival knives and spawned many imitators. The type has rather lost credibility over the years, owing to the many cheap and inferior hollow handled knives that were sold to unsuspecting users and failed to live up to expectations. The Jungle King II, however, remains a useful knife which is considerably stronger and more practical than many of its imitators.

The knife measures approximately 10 3/4in. long, with a 5 1/2in. hollow-ground Bowie type blade with a bellied main edge and a saw back. The bellied blade provides an effective reverse curve cutting edge, but the saw teeth are not so effective, clogging and jamming too easy to be very useful. The handle is an alloy tube, with chequered bands for grip. It has an integral double guard and screw-on butt cap which gives access to the compartment inside. This contains a basic survival kit of sticking plasters, safety pins, tweezers, pencil, sewing needles and thread, scalpel blade, fishing hooks, weights and line, and a flint striker.

The rigid plastic sheath is part of the 'system', incorporating a catapult, mini heliograph, sharpening stone, and 4m of black paracord. Basic ground-to-air signalling instructions are moulded into the plastic of the sheath. Also contained in the sheath is a small skinning knife/tool which has a 1 1/2in. main blade, gutting hook, shackle wrench, can/bottle opener and screwdriver.

The Jungle King II is often written off as a gimmicky survival knife, but it deserves more serious consideration: it is a surprisingly robust and practical tool which is perfectly capable of general camp and field tasks, with a useful array of survival items which would be welcome in an emergency.

Manufacturer:	Aitor Cuchilleria Del Norte SA, Ermua, Spain
Model:	Jungle King II
Length overall:	10 3/4in.
Blade length:	5 1/2in.
Blade shape:	Bowie, with bellied main edge
Blade material:	4mm thick chrome molybdenum vanadium stainless steel, 56-57 Rc
Edge:	Hollow-ground main edge, false clip edge, and 2 1/2in. saw toothed section on spine
Grip:	Black anodised alloy, tubular section, with chequered bands
Construction:	Short stub tang set into recess in handle
Sheath:	Green polyamide sheath with webbing belt loop, incorporating catapult, 4m paracord wrap, heliograph, sharpening stone and survival signalling instructions

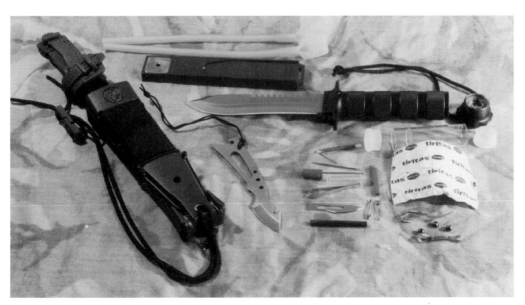

The knife universally known as the 'Ka-Bar' is the 1219C2 USMC Fighting/Utility knife which was first issued to US troops during the Second World War. Early models were manufactured by Union Cutlery under the Ka-Bar trademark, but over the years the knife has been made by several American companies, including Camillus, Case and Ontario, to Department of Defense specifications.

The background to this knife is covered in more depth earlier in this section, under the entry 'Camillus Marine Combat'

The Ka-Bar has a 6 7/8in. Bowie-type clip point blade, with a fuller or 'blood grove' on both sides. The clip edge is concave. The blade is made of carbon steel with a black protective finish. There is a straight double guard made of steel and the handle is made of brown leather washers stacked on the tang and held in place by a steel butt cap pinned through the end of the tang. This cap can be used as a light hammer.

The sheath is of brown leather, stitched and stapled, with the initials USMC and the US Marines globe, eagle and anchor symbol.

Manufacturer:	Ka-Bar Knives, part of Alcas Corp., Olean, New York, USA
Model:	USMC Fighting Knife
Length overall:	11 7/8in.
Blade length:	6 7/8in.
Blade shape:	Bowie with fuller
Blade material:	Carbon steel with protective black finish
Edge:	Bevel-ground, with false clip edge
Grip:	Brown leather, grooved, with steel butt-cap
Construction:	Stacked leather washers on full-length tang
Sheath:	Brown leather sheath with USMC logo

Ka-Bar developed their 'Next Generation' Fighting Knife as the successor to their famous USMC Fighting Knife, which has been a favourite of US servicemen for over 50 years. The Next Generation closely follows the dimensions and shape of the original Ka-Bar, but uses modern materials to provide superior performance and high resistance to corrosion.

The blade is made of high carbon stainless steel which is highly corrosion resistant. The handle is moulded Kraton, with a contoured shape and deep lateral grooves to improve the grip. The guard is single and is contoured to flow smoothly into the line of the handle. Likewise the stainless steel butt piece follows the curve of the handle and provides a surface for hammering as well as a lanyard hole.

The sheath has been brought up to date, too. It is made of moulded black Kydex in a rectangular shape and has a belt hanger and holes for a leg tie.

Manufacturer:	Ka-Bar Knives, part of Alcas Corp., Olean, New York, USA
Model:	Fighting Knife - The Next Generation
Length overall:	11 7/8in.
Blade length:	6 7/8in.
Blade shape:	Bowie
Blade material:	High carbon stainless steel
Edge:	Bevel-ground, with wave-form serrations on 1 3/4in. section near ricasso
Grip:	Moulded black Kraton rubber, contoured and grooved for grip
Construction:	Kraton grip fitted to full-length tang, with stainless steel single guard and butt
Sheath:	Black moulded Kydex belt sheath with leg tie

The MPK or Multi-Purpose Knife is unusual in that it is made of non-magnetic titanium alloy. It is used by US Navy SEALs and others for EOD work, as it will not affect magnetically-triggered 'influence mines'. The titanium alloy is also immensely strong, extremely resistant to corrosion, and holds a good edge, although it is so hard that it is unaffected by conventional sharpening stones and steels and must be sharpened with a special diamond hone.

The blade is 7 1/8in. long, and has a Bowie-type shape, although the clip is straight, resulting in a point almost of spear type. The edge is flat-ground, giving good cutting and slicing performance. While this type of grind is normally associated with a weaker blade, in this case the titanium is so strong that the problem does not arise. US Navy SEALs, notorious for giving their kit a hard time, used the knives for three years and never broke one. There is a 2in. serrated section near the handle which features special wave-form serrations designed to slice easily through rope, weed and the like.

The handle is made of high-performance Hytrel, a fire-resistant synthetic material, reinforced with Kevlar fibres. It is contoured to be held easily and firmly, even by a diver wearing gloves, and has longitudinal grooves for extra grip. The sheath is also made of Hytrel/Kevlar and has fittings so that it can be worn on a belt, strapped to a leg, or attached to webbing in an inverted position.

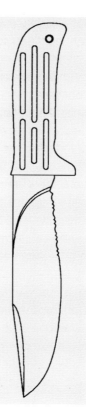

Manufacturer:	Mission Knives Inc., San Juan, California, USA
Model:	MPK
Length overall:	12 1/8in.
Blade length:	7 1/8in.
Blade shape:	Bowie with straight clip and bellied main edge
Blade material:	Mission Knives proprietary Beta-Titanium alloy
Edge:	Flat-grind, with wave-form serrations on 2in. section near handle
Grip:	Hytrel fire-resistant synthetic, reinforced with Kevlar, longitudinally grooved for grip
Construction:	Hytrel handle moulded on to full-length tang
Sheath:	Hytrel and Kevlar moulded sheath may be worn on belt, strapped to leg, or attached to webbing

The MoD Survival Knife is about as simple as a knife can be. It is basically a thick steel bar, with a sharpened edge at one end and wooden scales riveted on to the other to form a handle. The design is much like the British Army Golok, but with a shorter, stubbier blade.

It is a heavy, bulky knife, measuring 12 1/4in. long and weighing a little over 1lb 2oz. The blade is made of 1/4in. thick carbon steel, 7in. long and 1 5/8in. from spine to edge. The edge grind is quite steep, leaving plenty of meat in the blade for strength and heft. The weight is well forward, making this a good chopping and hammering tool, and the broad shape and strong tip make it excellent for digging and prying too. There is an oval double guard, which is spot welded to the tang at top and bottom.

The knife has a couple of drawbacks. First the handle, which is rather hard on the hands when used for heavy work: the large rivet holes, the less than perfect fit between wood and metal, and the lack of any vibration-absorbing ability combine to make this knife uncomfortable to use for extended periods with unprotected hands. Wrapping the handle with paracord helps to alleviate this and also provides a reserve supply of cordage for emergencies. Secondly, the knife is a purely heavy-duty

tool and is too clumsy for fine work. It really needs to be carried in conjunction with a Swiss Army Knife or Leatherman type multi-tool.

As a basic heavy chopper, this knife takes a lot of beating, however, and proves excellent at survival tasks from shelter building to digging a solar still or butchering large game. For these sorts of task, it is favoured by many of Britain's special forces.

Manufacturer:	Wilkinson Sword, England
Model:	Survival Knife
Length overall:	12 1/4in.
Blade length:	7in.
Blade shape:	Drop point
Blade material:	Carbon steel
Edge:	Bevel-ground
Grip:	Wooden scales
Construction:	Scales riveted to full tang with three large copper rivets
Sheath:	Simple brown leather sheath, stitched and riveted, with belt loop and press-studded retaining strap

This knife is Ontario's version of the Ka-Bar, officially designated the 1219C2 USMC Fighting/Utility knife, which was first issued to US troops during the Second World War. Ontario is one of several manufacturers who have made this knife to Department of Defense specifications.

The background to this knife is covered in more depth earlier, under the entry Camillus Marine Combat.

Manufacturer:	Ontario Knife Co., Franklinville, New York, USA
Model:	Marine Corps Combat Knife
Length overall:	12in.
Blade length:	7in.
Blade shape:	Bowie with blood groove. Saw back version available
Blade material:	Black-finished carbon steel
Edge:	Angle-grind
Grip:	Black leather
Construction:	Stacked leather washer handle secured by steel butt cap
Sheath:	Black leather belt sheath

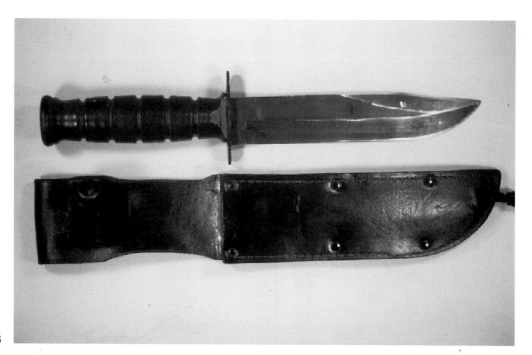

This knife is Ontario's version of the Navy Knife issued to US troops for many years. Ontario is one of several companies who have made this knife to Department of Defense specifications.

The knife is similar to the US Marine Corps Combat Knife, but has a number of differences to make it more suitable for use by the US Navy. The blade is made of stainless steel and finished with a protective black coating. The blade is shorter than that of the USMC Knife, at 6in., and has a pronounced concave sharpened clip edge which results in a very fine point. There is a saw back which is useful for cutting through weed, rope and the like.

Clearly a stacked leather washer handle would not survive long in marine conditions, and on the Navy Knife the handle is made of moulded black plastic pieces, contoured and chequered for grip and screwed to the full-length tang.

The sheath is made of rigid black plastic, with a Cordura hanger and a clip for a military web belt.

Manufacturer:	Ontario Knife Co., Franklinville, New York, USA
Model:	Navy Knife
Length overall:	10 7/8in.
Blade length:	6in.
Blade shape:	Bowie with serrated back and deep clip
Blade material:	Black finished stainless steel
Edge:	Angle-grind
Grip:	Moulded black plastic
Construction:	Grip screwed through tang
Sheath:	US Navy issue knife

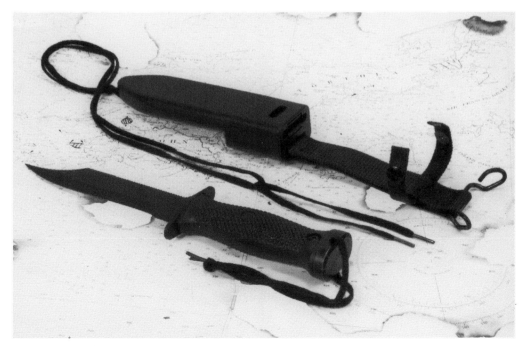

This knife is Ontario's version of the Pilot Survival Knife issued to US aircrew for many years. The company is one of a number who have made this knife to American Government specifications.

The background to this knife is covered in more depth earlier, under the entry Camillus Pilot Survival.

Manufacturer:	Ontario Knife Co., Franklinville, New York, USA
Model:	Air Force Survival Knife
Length overall:	9 1/2in.
Blade length:	5in.
Blade shape:	Bowie-style with blood groove, deep belly and saw back
Blade material:	Black finished carbon steel
Edge:	Angle-grind
Grip:	Natural leather
Construction:	Leather washer handle secured by pommel
Sheath:	Natural leather sheath with sharpening stone pocket

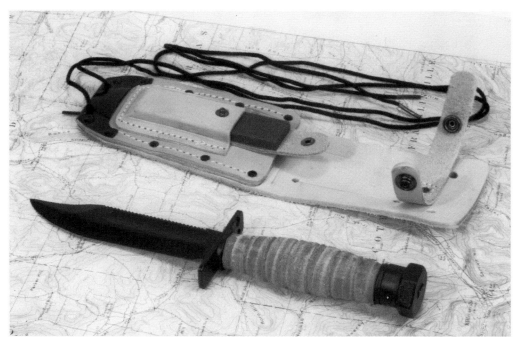

The SOG Bowie is the company's original flagship model and was developed for the US 5th Special Forces in the Vietnam War for reconnaissance, infiltration and behind-the-lines operations.

The knife measures 10 3/4in. overall, with a blade of unusually thick (0.28in.) SK5 carbon tool steel hardened to Rc 57-58. The main edge has a deep hollow grind and there is a distinctive double concave clip on the back edge. The tip is faceted to give superb penetration and fine point work. The blade is engraved with the crest and logo of US Special Forces in Vietnam.

The handle is made of stacked leather washers, with white fibre spacers at either end. The double guard and butt are made of blued steel and are contoured to follow the lines of the grip. This gives the knife a more comfortable grip, as well as adding to its fine looks.

Manufacturer:	SOG Knives, Edmonds, Washington, USA
Model:	Bowie
Length overall:	10 3/4in.
Blade length:	6 1/4in.
Blade shape:	Bowie
Blade material:	SK-5 carbon tool steel, with blued finish
Edge:	Hollow-ground; false back edge
Grip:	Natural leather
Construction:	Stacked leather washer grip on full-length tang; blued steel crossguard and butt, held in place by aircraft spanner nut
Sheath:	Leather pouch with sharpening stone

The SOG Government model is a Bowie-type knife with a 6 1/4in. blade of 440A stainless steel and a chequered Kraton handle (Kraton has a slightly 'tacky' feel in wet conditions, and tends to adhere to the hand, giving a sure grip). The crossguard and pommel are of stainless steel, and the guard is soldered to the blade to keep out moisture. The blade is bevel-ground with a straight clip.

The SOG Government is a straightforward design which uses advanced materials for superior performance. It is a good, all-round, field knife, which is capable of being used as a fighter if necessary.

Manufacturer:	SOG Knives, Edmonds, Washington, USA
Model:	Government (Recon Government version available with deep blued finish to all metal parts)
Length overall:	11 1/4in.
Blade length:	6 1/4in.
Blade shape:	Bowie
Blade material:	440-A stainless steel, Rc 57-58
Edge:	Bevel-ground
Grip:	One-piece Kraton grip with wrap-round chequering
Construction:	Full-length tang
Sheath:	Nylon belt sheath

Designed for the US Navy SEALs, the SOG Seal Knife 2000 is a strong, high-performance knife which is highly resistant to sea water. It measures 12 1/4in. overall, with a 7in. Parkerised 440-A stainless steel blade hardened to Rc 55-56. The blade shape is along similar lines to SOG's successful Bowie and Trident models, with a double concave clip which extends almost the full length of the back edge. There is a 1 1/2in. serrated section on the main edge near the hilt.

The handle is made of contoured black Zytel, with chequering and finger grooves for grip and an integral guard. The knife comes with a black nylon belt sheath with leg tie.

Manufacturer:	SOG Knives, Edmonds, Washington, USA
Model:	SEAL Knife 2000
Length overall:	12 1/4in.
Blade length:	7in.
Blade shape:	Bowie with double concave clip
Blade material:	1/4in. thick 440-A stainless steel, Rc 55-56, Parkerised
Edge:	Bevel-ground, with 1 1/2in. serrated section near hilt
Grip:	One-piece Kraton grip with chequering and finger grooves
Construction:	Handle moulded to full-length tang
Sheath:	Black nylon belt sheath with leg tie

The SOG Tech is a knife that combines an established blade and handle shape with modern materials for good looks and performance. There are two models, the 5 3/4in. blade Tech I, and the 7 1/4in. blade Tech II. Both models feature the double concave clip blade seen on SOG's highly respected Bowie and Trident models.

The handles are of contoured black Kraton rubber, with a chequered non-slip surface, and brass guard. Each knife comes with a black nylon belt sheath, with leg tie.

These are multi-purpose knives which may be used for most field tasks and will also serve as effective fighters when circumstances require.

Manufacturer:	SOG Knives, Edmonds, Washington, USA
Model:	SOG-Tech II (SOG-Tech I similar but 11in. overall, and with 6in. blade)
Length overall:	12 1/2in.
Blade length:	7 1/4in.
Blade shape:	Clip point
Blade material:	1/4in. thick 440-A stainless steel, Rc 56-57
Edge:	Bevel-ground
Grip:	One-piece Kraton grip with wrap-round chequering and lanyard hole
Construction:	Full-length tang construction, with brass crossguard
Sheath:	Nylon scabbard

The SOG Tigershark follows the same lines as the company's famous Bowie and Trident models, but is considerably larger at 14in. overall with a 9in. carbon steel blade. It has a one-piece, contoured Kraton rubber handle, with integral double guard and non-slip chequered surface.

This is a big, powerful knife that offers useful chopping, hacking and slashing performance, while remaining capable of more delicate work. Penetration by the sharply pointed tip is excellent.

The Tigershark is a versatile knife which will cope admirably with most tasks requiring a big knife, and makes a formidable fighter as well as a highly effective combat survival knife. It is also available with a gun-blue finish as the Midnite Tiger.

Manufacturer:	SOG Knives, Edmonds, Washington, USA
Model:	Tigershark
Length overall:	14in.
Blade length:	9in.
Blade shape:	Clip point
Blade material:	1/4in. thick carbon steel, Rc 56-57
Edge:	Bevel-ground
Grip:	Moulded Kraton grip with wrap-round chequering and lanyard hole
Construction:	Handle moulded to full-length tang
Sheath:	Nylon belt sheath

The SOG Trident is a development of the company's renowned Bowie, with almost identical dimensions and lines. However, it makes use of more modern materials for better all-round performance and resistance to corrosion.

The blade is hand ground from 440C stainless steel, hardened to Rc 57-58. The handle is black micarta with white spacers, and the contoured double guard and pommel are of stainless steel. The knife comes with a waterproof black nylon sheath with leg tie.

Manufacturer: SOG Knives, Edmonds, Washington, USA

Model: Trident

Length overall: 10 3/4in.

Blade length: 6 1/4in.

Blade shape: Clip point

Blade material: 0.28in. thick 440-C stainless steel, Rc 57-58

Edge: 'Surgical'-ground, faceted tip

Grip: Stacked Micarta handle, steel pommel with lanyard hole

Construction: Full-length tang construction

Sheath: Nylon scabbard

Ontario Knife Co. are one of a number of manufacturers who make the US forces issue knives such as the Marine Combat, Air Force Survival and Navy Knives.

Spec Plus is the company's vision of the next generation of military knives, offering the same proven blade shapes but with improved handles of Kraton rubber, with integral guards. Blade material is generally thicker and the general standard of construction higher than with standard issue knives.

This is the Spec Plus version of the Marine Combat Knife, with the same fullered Bowie blade, but in a thicker (3/16in.) steel, and with a contoured Kraton handle. It comes with a black nylon belt sheath.

Manufacturer:	Ontario Knife Co., Franklinville, New York, USA
Model:	SP1 Marine Combat
Length overall:	12 1/8in.
Blade length:	7in.. Blade depth 1 1/4in.
Blade shape:	Bowie with blood groove
Blade material:	3/16in. thick 1095 carbon steel, black epoxy powder coated
Edge:	Bevel-ground
Grip:	Black Kraton grooved handle with lanyard hole
Construction:	Handle moulded on to full-length tang
Sheath:	Black nylon belt sheath

The SP2 is the Spec Plus version of the Air Force Survival Knife, with the same fullered Bowie blade shape and saw back, but deeper at 1 1/4in., and made from a thicker (3/16in.) steel. It has a contoured Kraton handle, and comes with a black nylon belt sheath.

Manufacturer:	Ontario Knife Co., Franklinville, New York, USA
Model:	SP2 Air Force Survival
Length overall:	10 5/8in.
Blade length:	5 1/2in.
Blade shape:	Bowie, with saw back and blood groove
Blade material:	3/16in. thick 1095 carbon steel, black epoxy powder coated
Edge:	Bevel-ground
Grip:	Black Kraton grooved handle with lanyard hole
Construction:	Handle moulded on to full-length tang
Sheath:	Black nylon belt sheath

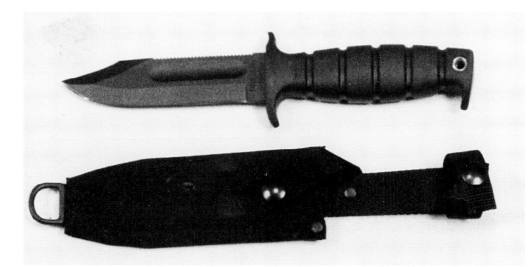

The SP3 is the Spec Plus version of the Trench Knife based on the M7 bayonet. It has the same spear-point blade shape with half-length sharpened back edge, but is made from thicker (3/16in.) steel and has a contoured Kraton handle with integral double guard.

The knife has a sharply pointed, steel 'skull crusher' pommel, which is black powder coated. This feature is felt by some to be useful in close combat, but may give the user a nasty poke if he sits down carelessly with the knife in a belt sheath. Some users take a file and round off the point.

Manufacturer:	Ontario Knife Co., Franklinville, New York, USA
Model:	SP3 M7 Bayonet Knife
Length overall:	12 1/2in.
Blade length:	6 3/4in.
Blade shape:	Spear point
Blade material:	3/16in. thick 1095 carbon steel, black epoxy powder coated
Edge:	Bevel-ground
Grip:	Black Kraton grooved handle with 'skull crusher' pommel
Construction:	Moulded Kraton handle; pommel screwed to tang
Sheath:	Black Cordura belt sheath

The SP4 is the Spec Plus version of the Navy Knife, with the same concave clip Bowie blade shape and serrated back, but made from thicker (3/16in.) 440A stainless steel. It has a contoured Kraton handle with integral double guard, and comes with a black nylon belt sheath.

Manufacturer:	Ontario Knife Co., Franklinville, New York, USA
Model:	SP4 Navy Knife
Length overall:	11 1/8in.
Blade length:	6in.
Blade shape:	Bowie, with serrated back and deep clip
Blade material:	3/16in. thick 440A stainless steel, black epoxy powder coated
Edge:	Bevel-ground
Grip:	Black Kraton grooved handle with lanyard hole
Construction:	Kraton handle moulded on to tang
Sheath:	Black Cordura belt sheath

The Spec Plus Survival Bowie is a massive blade with dimensions and handling more like those of a machete than a knife. It has a flat ground 10in. blade of 1/4in. thick 1095 carbon steel, with an upturned clip point. Overall the knife measures 15 1/8in. from tip to butt. The heavy, flat-ground blade has immense cutting and chopping power, and makes short work of dense brush and undergrowth. Despite its size, this big Bowie is also capable of remarkably delicate work. It slices well, and the point is quite fine.

Although not its main purpose, this knife would also make an effective fighting weapon, with good stand-off, an intimidating appearance, and the ability to stab, slash and cut.

Like all the Spec Plus range, the Survival Bowie has a moulded Kraton handle, with integral guard and deep lateral grooves for extra grip. It comes with a Cordura sheath with a leather belt loop attached to a pivot ring, and there is a loop at the tip for a leg tie.

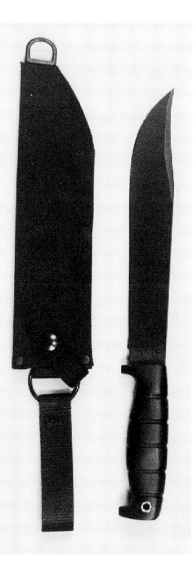

Manufacturer:	Ontario Knife Co., Franklinville, New York, USA
Model:	SP5 Survival Bowie
Length overall:	15 1/8in.
Blade length:	10in.
Blade shape:	Bowie
Blade material:	1/4in. thick 1095 carbon steel, black epoxy powder coated
Edge:	Flat-ground, with concave false clip edge
Grip:	Black Kraton grooved handle with lanyard hole
Construction:	Handle moulded on to full-length tang
Sheath:	Cordura sheath with pivot ring and tie cord

The Spec Plus SP6 Fighting Knife is based on the Randall R1 blade shape described earlier, under the heading Blackjack Model 1-7. A proven and versatile design, it works well in the Spec Plus guise, with a black epoxy coating and moulded Kraton handle.

This is a big, powerful knife, with an 8in. blade and measuring 13 1/8in. overall. The blade is 3/16in. thick, and has a sharpened straight clip edge. Like the other Spec Plus knives, it has a bellied handle with deep grooves for added grip.

Although described as a fighter, this knife is much more versatile, with the ability to cope well with medium chopping, slashing, cutting and piercing. It makes a useful field tool.

Manufacturer:	Ontario Knife Co., Franklinville, New York, USA
Model:	SP6 Fighting Knife
Length overall:	13 1/8in.
Blade length:	8in.
Blade shape:	Randall R1 type straight clip Bowie
Blade material:	1/4in. thick 1095 carbon steel, black epoxy powder coated
Edge:	Bevel ground
Grip:	Black Kraton grooved handle with lanyard hole
Construction:	Handle moulded on to full-length tang
Sheath:	Cordura belt sheath

The Spec Plus SPC20 USMC Parachutist knife and SPC21 Navy Mark 1 are relatively recent additions to the Spec Plus range. They mark a departure from the established Spec Plus look, with bright brush finished metalwork rather than the deliberately sombre black powder coating that had come to be associated with these knives.

The quality is entirely characteristic of Spec Plus, however, with a 1095 carbon steel blade, full-length tang, and contoured moulded Kraton handle with the familiar bellied shape, deep lateral grooves and integral double guard.

The USMC Parachutist has a straight clipped, flat ground blade, with a tip that is almost a spear point. The blade is relatively small, at 4 1/8in. long, with a thickness of 1/6in.. It is a handy utility blade, good for cutting and piercing, but does not have the size and heft to tackle heavy chopping and slicing. For cutting tangled parachute cords it would be ideal.

The Navy Mark 1 is very similar, but with a slightly longer 4 3/4in. blade, giving it an overall length of 9 1/4in.. The extra length makes this knife slightly more versatile, but it is still not enough to allow for heavy work.

The Kraton handle is common to both knives. It gives good grip and flares to a milled butt cap which is screwed on to the full-length tang. This can be used for hammering and pounding

Manufacturer:	Ontario Knife Co., Franklinville, New York, USA
Model:	SPS20 USMC Parachutist/SPC21 Navy Mark 1
Length overall:	8 3/4in./9 3/4in.
Blade length:	4in./4 3/4in.
Blade shape:	Straight clip point with false top edge
Blade material:	1/6in. thick 1095 carbon steel with bright brushed finish
Edge:	Flat-grind
Grip:	Black Kraton grooved handle
Construction:	Stainless steel butt cap screwed on to threaded tang
Sheath:	Leather and Cordura belt sheath with leg tie

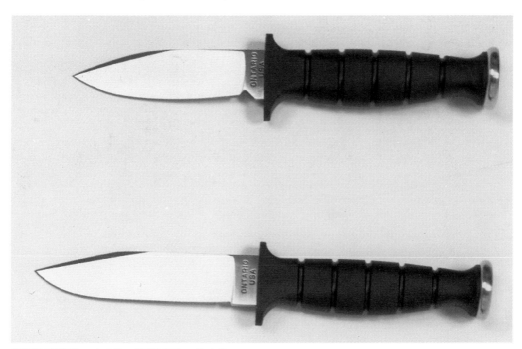

'SPC 20 USMC Parachutist' and 'SPC 21 Navy Mark 1'.

Like the USMC Parachutist and Navy Mark 1, the Patrol and Ranger stand apart from the rest of the Spec Plus range, owing to their bright brushed blades and butt caps.

The two knives differ in blade shape only. The Patrol has a spear point blade which is basically a shortened version of the M7 bayonet, while the Ranger's blade is a straight clip Bowie-style. Both blades are made of 1/6in. thick 1095 carbon steel.

The handles are identical, made of Kraton rubber moulded to a contoured shape that incorporates deep lateral grooves and double guards. The handles flare at the butt to accommodate the butt cap, which is screwed on to the full-length, threaded tang.

Manufacturer:	Ontario Knife Co., Franklinville, New York, USA
Model:	SPC22 Patrol/SPC23 Ranger
Length overall:	9 3/4in.
Blade length:	5in.
Blade shape:	Spear point/straight clip Bowie
Blade material:	1/6in. thick 1095 carbon steel with bright brushed finish
Edge:	Bevel-ground
Grip:	Moulded Kraton rubber, contoured, with grooves and integral double guard
Construction:	Steel butt cap screwed on to threaded end of full-length tang
Sheath:	Black Cordura and leather belt sheath with lanyard

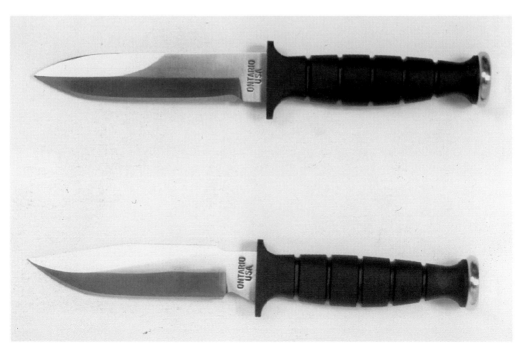

The Timberline Specwar knife was designed by Ernest Emerson to meet US Special Warfare Group specifications. It is a high-tech knife, made of modern, high-performance materials, and with an unusual blade and handle profile. This is not what some would call an attractive knife to look at, but its performance is exceptional.

The blade is angular, with a clipped chisel point reminiscent of the Tanto shape, and a straight main edge. The grind is one side of the blade only, giving good strength and cutting efficiency. The chisel point has exceptional penetration and may also be used for quite fine work when necessary. The blade material is ATS-34 steel and unusually hard at Rc 60.

The handle is contoured nylon, with a belly and single guard. The top edge extends well along the back of the blade, allowing one to place the thumb well forward to exert a powerful downward cutting pressure. There is a deep finger groove choil, so that one may choke up the grip for fine work, and the shape of the butt allows the grip to be extended for hacking and slashing.

This is an unusual, futuristic-looking knife which develops some interesting ideas and offers outstanding performance in important areas. It is perhaps a little specialised for general field use, but would tackle most camp chores with ease and could also serve well as a fighter if necessary. It is available with either a grey bead blasted finish, or black titanium nitride coating.

Manufacturer:	Timberline, USA
Model:	Specwar
Length overall:	11 7/8in.
Blade length:	6in.
Blade shape:	Chisel point
Blade material:	ATS-34 stainless steel, Rc 60, with bead blasted grey finish or black titanium nitride coating
Edge:	Bevel-ground one side only
Grip:	Moulded black nylon
Construction:	Nylon handle moulded to full-length tang
Sheath:	Rigid Kydex sheath with 'jump safe' features

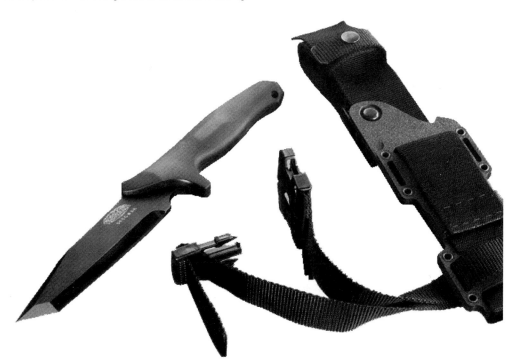

The United Special Operations Utility Knife is an unusual design, consisting of a single flat piece of ATS-34 stainless steel machined to form a blade and handle. The blade is a spear point design, with a convex main blade and a sharpened back edge with serrations cut into it. The serrations are, in fact, notches which do not need sharpening individually - the blade is simply sharpened on a flat hone.

The handle is a skeleton design, simply shaped from the full tang of the knife. It has two finger grooves, and the tang is drilled through in four places. These holes serve to lighten the knife, as well as providing a means of lashing it to a pole to form a spear. A smaller hole at the butt end allows one to attach a lanyard. Also in the butt is a notch for cutting wire. This is not so much a wire cutter as a wire breaker, and is claimed to work on wire up to 1/8in. thick.

The sheath is made of black nylon web, with a rigid plastic insert that is held in place by a Velcro strip, allowing it to be removed if required. The sheath allows various carrying options: it may be attached to a belt with a loop or Alice clips, worn on a leg or arm with rubber diving straps, or attached to webbing via the six impact resistant grommets.

Manufacturer:	United Cutlery, Sevierville, Tennessee, USA
Model:	Special Ops Utility Knife
Length overall:	8 7/8in.
Blade length:	4 3/8in.
Blade shape:	Spear point
Blade material:	ATS-34 stainless steel with black finish
Edge:	Bevel-ground main edge, serrated back edge
Grip:	Bare full tang with finger grooves
Construction:	Single piece of steel, ground and milled to shape
Sheath:	Black nylon web sheath with removable plastic insert

MULTI-TOOLS

The Multi-Plier is Gerber's answer to the various multi-tools that have appeared in recent years, but it is not just a copycat item - it brings some completely new ideas of its own to answer the challenge of cramming as many tools as possible into a pocket-sized package.

Most multi-tools fold the plier head away into the handle, in the manner of the Leatherman, whereas the Gerber's Multi-Plier has a unique sliding mechanism, so that the plier head retracts into the handles when not in use. This makes the pliers easy to deploy with a quick flick of the wrist, with centrifugal force throwing the plier head out until the sprung buttons lock in place. The mechanism also means that the handles are not reversed when using the pliers, so the palm of the hand presses against the rounded outside edge of the handles - a feature that makes the pliers more comfortable to use than some other types. The tool is designed so that the handles cannot quite come together when the pliers are in use, preventing any painful trapping of a fold of skin between the handles. The Multi-Plier is available with either square-ended or needlenose pliers.

The other tools are located in the handles, hinged at the bottom end of each in the same way as a folding knife blade. There are two main blades, both 2 5/8in. long - one a drop point, the other a serrated sheepsfoot type. Also in the handles are three straight screwdriver blades, a Phillips screwdriver, a metal file, a fold-out lanyard ring, and a can/bottle opener. The tools all click into place with an over-centre spring mechanism, but do not lock. With the handles held together, however, the blades are able to fold only partly, and cannot close on to the hand holding the tool. The handles are marked in inches and centimetres for measuring up to 3in. or 7cm.

The Multi-Tool comes in a black ballistic nylon belt pouch. As an optional accessory, one may also buy a tool kit which includes an adapter that fits on the Phillips screwdriver, together with a selection of 1/4in. hex bits for several screw head types.

Having tested all the various multi-tools available, I have carried a Gerber Multi-Plier for the past two years in preference to other models. It is not always the strongest, lightest, most powerful or easiest to use, but

I have found that it offers the best compromise. The deciding factor was the ease and speed with which the plier head can be deployed, even with only one hand free.

Manufacturer:	Gerber (a division of Fiskars Inc.), Portland, Oregon, USA
Model:	G-55800 Multi-Plier
Length overall:	4 3/8in. (closed), 6in. (open)
Blade length:	2 5/8in. main and serrated blades
Blade shape:	Drop point main blade, sheepsfoot serrated blade
Blade material:	All stainless steel, bead blasted finish (black finish version available)
Edge:	Hollow-ground
Grip:	Plier handles form grip
Construction:	Slide-out pliers with hinged knife blades and tools in handles
Features:	Pliers (needlenose or square-ended versions available) with wire cutter, file, three straight-head screwdrivers, Phillips screwdriver, lanyard ring, can/bottle opener, blades as above, ruler, black ballistic nylon belt pouch. Supplementary tool kit available with coupler and assorted screwdriver heads in pouch

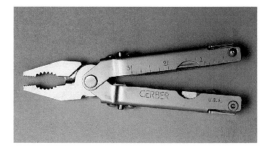

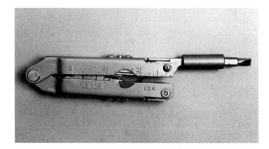

Gerber's MPT, or Military Provisional Tool, was developed to meet a US military specification. Unlike the company's Multi-Plier, the MPT follows the Leatherman design in which the plier handles are hinged on the base of the pliers and fold out for use. This means the edges of the U-section handles bear on the palm of the hand and so Gerber have folded these edges to increase the surface area in contact with the hand in an attempt to make them more comfortable to use. Like the Multi-Plier, the plier jaws of the MPT are narrower than those in some other tools, but are still strong enough for most jobs. I have used the MPT and prefer the Multi-Plier or the Leatherman - but to be fair the MPT is a rugged and effective tool made to tight price constraints. It has been adopted by a number of US and other military forces.

Manufacturer: Gerber (a division of Fiskars Inc.), Portland, Oregon, USA

Model: MPT (Military Provisional Tool)

Length overall: 4 1/2in. closed

Blade length: 2 5/8in.

Blade shape: Drop point main blade

Blade material: All stainless steel, bead blasted finish (Black finish version available)

Edge: Hollow-ground

Grip: Plier handles form grip

Construction: Folding construction with hinged knife blades and tools in handles

Features: Needlenose pliers with wire cutter, file, two straight-head screwdrivers, Phillips screwdriver, lanyard ring, can/bottle opener, main blade as above, small utility blade, ruler

The Leatherman Tool was the original multi-tool - the first tool, to my knowledge, to apply the principle of a folding plier with tools and blades located in the handles. Certainly it was the one that popularised the multi-tool idea and spawned numerous imitators.

Although other models have come along, the original Leatherman Tool is still hugely popular, both with military personnel and civilians. It consists of a plier head with two U-section stainless steel handles. These fold around a hinge pin near the plier head, so that they completely enclose the plier head when closed. The plier head is the needlenose type and incorporates a wire cutter. One minor drawback of the design is that, when using the pliers, the open side of the U is against the palm, which makes it uncomfortable to use force on the work.

Hinged at the bottom end of the handles are a selection of tools: a hollow-ground clip point blade, a metal file, three sizes of slot-head screwdriver, a Phillips screwdriver, an awl, and a can/bottle opener. The tools are held in place by an overcentre flat spring when opened, but do not lock. However they cannot close on the hand when in use, as they are stopped by the opposing handle.

On the outer edge of the handles is a ruler scale marked in centimetres and inches and by aligning the handles in the partly folded position the scale will measure up to 20cm or 8in..

The Leatherman Tool comes with either a leather or ballistic nylon belt pouch, and has a lanyard ring attachment.

The original Leatherman is a simple and effective tool which packs enormous versatility into a small space. It is still deservedly one of the most popular multi-tools and is an ideal addition to a survival kit or tool kit.

It is available in either bright stainless steel or a black finish. There is also a military version, with a detonator crimp tool incorporated into the plier head, which has proved popular with combat engineers, ATOs and EOD.

Manufacturer:	Leatherman Tool Group Inc., Portland, Oregon, USA
Model:	Leatherman Tool
Length overall:	4in. (closed)
Blade length:	2 5/8in.
Blade shape:	Clip point
Blade material:	All stainless steel, satin finish (also available in black finish)
Edge:	Hollow-ground main blade
Grip:	Plier handles form grip
Construction:	Folding construction with hinged knife blades and tools in handles
Features:	Needlenose pliers with wire cutter, main blade as above, ruler, can/bottle opener, three sizes of slot-head screwdriver, Phillips screwdriver, file with saw-type edge, awl, leather belt sheath

Leatherman's Mini Tool takes the already small, original Leatherman and makes it smaller still - just 2 5/8in. long when closed. This was achieved by having the handles fold in half before closing them on to the plier head - a second piece of U-section handle folds into the first. This restricts the space available for tools in the handle, but even so Leatherman have managed to fit in a hollow-ground clip blade and a file/screwdriver. The handle extensions incorporate a can opener and a bottle opener.

The Mini Tool comes in bright stainless or black finish and has a small ballistic nylon belt pouch. Although the selection of tools is limited, and the small size restricts the power of the pliers, it is still a robust and practical tool and is useful where space is limited - in a belt-mounted survival pack, for instance.

Manufacturer:	Leatherman Tool Group Inc., Portland, Oregon, USA
Model:	Mini Tool
Length overall:	2 5/8in. (closed)
Blade length:	1 1/2in.
Blade shape:	Clip point
Blade material:	All stainless steel, satin finish (also available in black finish)
Edge:	Hollow-ground main blade
Grip:	Plier handles form grip
Construction:	Double folding construction with hinged knife blades and tools in handles
Features:	Needlenose pliers with wire cutter, main blade as above, ruler, can opener, bottle opener, file with screwdriver tip, black Cordura belt sheath

Based on the original Leatherman Tool, the PST II (Pocket Survival Tool II) offers an uprated tool selection in the same sized package. Like the original tool, the PST II has a needlenose plier head with wire cutters and folding U-section handles. Tools in the handles include the familiar Phillips and slot-head screwdrivers and can/bottle opener. In addition, however, the PST II has a very sharp serrated main clip blade, scissors and a diamond-coated crosscut file with a sharpening groove for needles, fish hooks and the like.

One of the few complaints about the original Leatherman was its lack of scissors, which are more suitable for some fine cutting jobs than a knife blade. The PST II puts this right and at the same time offers an uprated file and main blade - the serrated section is very effective in cutting tough materials such as rope and webbing.

These improvements have been achieved within the same overall size as the original Leatherman, at just 4in. x 1in. x 7/16in. when closed, making it a very handy, lightweight and versatile item. It is available with a leather or ballistic nylon belt pouch.

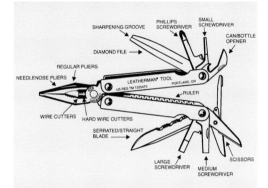

Manufacturer:	Leatherman Tool Group Inc., Portland, Oregon, USA
Model:	PST II
Length overall:	4in. (closed), 6 1/4in. (open)
Blade length:	2 5/8in.
Blade shape:	Clip point with serrated section
Blade material:	All stainless steel, satin finish
Edge:	Hollow-ground, with serrated section
Grip:	Plier handles form grip
Construction:	Folding construction with hinged knife blades and tools in handles
Features:	Needlenose pliers with wire cutter, main blade as above, scissors, ruler, can/bottle opener, three sizes of slot-head screwdriver, Phillips screwdriver, file with diamond-coated side and cross-cut side, awl, leather belt sheath

The original Leatherman Tool was such a useful and practical item that it was inevitable that people would ask for more - more power, more tools and more features. These could be provided only at the expense of greater bulk and weight, but for some users a bigger, heavier tool was acceptable if it would tackle heavier work.

The Supertool addressed this by offering a number of extra items, notably a second blade with a very effective serrated edge, and a high-performance wood/bone saw. Making the tool bigger also allowed the plier head and other tools to be bulked up, offering more power and strength to cope with heavier work.

The other major addition in the Supertool was a locking mechanism on all the fold-out tools and blades. This is achieved with a catch in the spring back, which engages in a notch on each blade when it is fully opened. The blade is then held firmly in the open position and cannot fold regardless of the direction of the force on it. This is particularly valuable for the knife and screwdriver blades, which in the original Leatherman may fold suddenly when force is applied to the work.

The downside is that releasing the locking mechanism may be fiddly. This requires one to open another blade in the same handle half-way - raising the

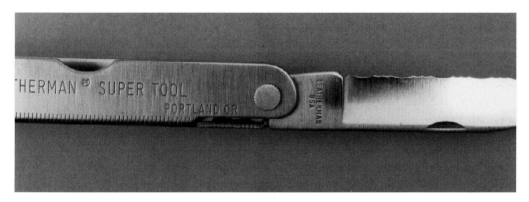

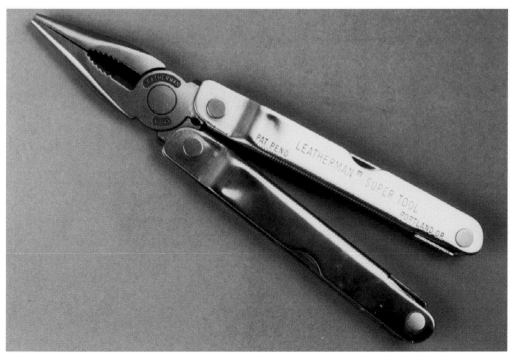

catch out of the notch and allowing both blades to be closed. In practice this may be awkward, not to mention risky with cold, slippery hands, since one is opening the second blade towards an open sharp edge. Provided that this is done carefully there is no need for a mishap, however, and in two years of using the Supertool I have not had an accident - indeed, it becomes easier as the blades wear and the hinge mechanism frees up.

The Supertool is altogether bigger and heavier than the original Leatherman, at 4 1/2in. x 1 1/4in. x 5/8in. With heavier work, however, the extra weight and bulk are well worth it - the tools are better able to cope and the locking mechanism makes the job safer. The wood saw in particular is valuable outdoors, cutting branches for a shelter or trap with ease - something that would not be possible with a standard multi-tool. The knife blades are big and strong enough to dress medium-sized game, and would even serve for fighting in a dire emergency. If one is going to depend on a multi-tool alone for survival then the Supertool is the one to choose.

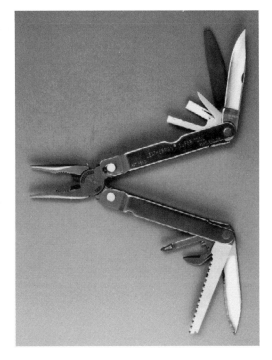

Manufacturer:	Leatherman Tool Group Inc., Portland, Oregon, USA
Model:	Supertool
Length overall:	4 1/2in. (closed)
Blade length:	3in.
Blade shape:	Clip point main blade, drop point serrated blade
Blade material:	All stainless steel, satin finish
Edge:	Hollow-ground
Grip:	Plier handles form grip
Construction:	Folding construction with locking hinged knife blades and tools in handles
Features:	Needlenose pliers with wire cutter and wire crimper, main blades as above, wood saw, ruler, can/bottle opener, file, three sizes of slot-head screwdriver, Phillips screwdriver, awl, brown leather belt pouch

The Mauser Officer's Knife is made under licence by Victorinox of Switzerland - makers of the famous Swiss Army Knives. A simple folding pocket knife, it incorporates a few extras that bring it into the multi-tool category.

The knife measures 4 1/4in. long and has green plastic scales with moulded chequering for extra grip. There are two main blades - a flat-ground drop point blade, and a clip point, also flat-ground, which bears the Mauser logo and text which declares that the Mauser name is being used under licence.

Next to the main blades is a third, of the same length, which has a 2 1/4in. saw edge, plus a bottle opener and a screwdriver at the tip. The saw teeth are very aggressive, and set alternately right and left to remove material to the thickness of the blade, so the saw does not jam as it cuts through wood or bone. This saw is extremely effective on softwood and will even do a decent job on hardwood, although it is inclined to bite too deep if any downward pressure is applied. Its only real drawback is its length, which means that one may only use very short strokes. The saw comes with a thin metal cover to protect the fingers when using the bottle opener or screwdriver on the same blade.

On the back of the knife are an awl/reamer and a corkscrew. There is a hole through one end of the knife where a lanyard may be attached.

A good, sturdy, pocket knife with an impressive saw blade, the Mauser Officer's Knife nevertheless offers fewer tools than the equivalently sized Swiss Army Knives and has never become a very popular private purchase item for the military.

Manufacturer:	Victorinox, Switzerland
Model:	Mauser Officer's Knife
Length overall:	4 1/4in. (closed)
Blade length:	3 1/4in.
Blade shape:	One drop point blade, one clip
Blade material:	Stainless steel
Edge:	Flat-ground (both blades)
Grip:	Green plastic scales with moulded chequering
Construction:	Standard folding pocket knife construction, with blades sandwiched between metal scales held by pins
Features:	Two blades as above, wood saw/bottle opener/screwdriver blade, awl/reamer, corkscrew, lanyard hole

SOG's development of the Leatherman idea was the ParaTool. Designed by Blackie Collins and Spencer Frazer, it is a folding plier/multi-tool with some innovative ideas. For a start, the handles do not have to be folded round to expose the plier head. Instead, the plier head is hinged sideways in the handles, and is flipped into position by pressing on a tab which doubles as a lanyard ring. This enables one to deploy the pliers single handedly, which is useful when one hand is occupied. The design also means that the palm of the hand is pressing against the rounded side of the U-section

handles, which gives greater comfort than some other multi-tool designs. The handle surfaces are drilled with a pattern of small holes to give a better grip.

The selection of tools is a good one, with a 3in. straight blade, 3in. serrated sheepsfoot blade, file, three slot-head screwdrivers, a Phillips screwdriver, a can/bottle opener, an awl, and a coarse/fine file. Unlike other multi-tools of this type, the SOG ParaTool's hinge pins have hex heads, and may be unscrewed so that the user can alter the tool configuration – optional accessory blades include a seat belt/gutting hook and a double tooth wood/bone saw.

The ParaTool has an injection moulded black plastic belt pouch with a locking mechanism to prevent the tool falling out while being carried.

Manufacturer:	SOG Speciality Knives Inc., Edmonds, Washington, USA
Model:	ParaTool
Length overall:	4in. closed, 6 2/5in. open
Blade length:	3in. standard blade, 3in. serrated blade
Blade shape:	Drop point standard blade, sheepsfoot serrated blade
Blade material:	420 stainless steel, satin finish, also available in black finish
Edge:	Hollow-ground
Grip:	Plier handles form grip
Construction:	Folding construction with hinged knife blades and tools
Features:	Needlenose pliers with wire cutter, three sizes of flathead screwdriver, Phillips screwdriver, metal file, awl, can/bottle opener, ruler, lanyard hole and two blades as above. Optional saw blade and seat belt cutter/gutting blade. Moulded plastic belt sheath

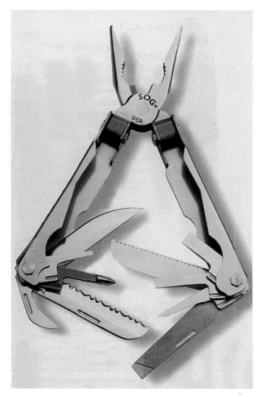

With the Power Plier, SOG have reverted to the folding-handle system pioneered by Leatherman, but have built in a gear mechanism that increases the leverage on the plier head. The Power Plier has similar tools to the ParaTool, and the same hex bolt construction that allows one to add optional blades and to adjust the ease of opening to the personal preference.

The main blade is a drop point with a partially serrated edge; other tools are the same as those in the ParaTool, and are listed below. The Power Plier comes with a heavy duty nylon belt pouch.

A smaller version, the Mini Pocket Power Plier, is also available, measuring 4in. when closed. This has fewer blades but retains the main blade, two slot-head screwdrivers, Phillips screwdriver, can/bottle opener, and file.

Manufacturer:	SOG Speciality Knives Inc., Edmonds, Washington, USA
Model:	Power Plier
Length overall:	4 1/4in. x 1/4in. x 5/8in. (closed), length 6 3/4in. (open)
Blade length:	3in.
Blade shape:	Drop point blade with serrated section
Blade material:	All stainless steel, polished finish
Edge:	Hollow-ground
Grip:	Plier handles form grip
Construction:	Folding construction with hinged knife blades and tools. Gear mechanism provides added leverage for pliers
Features:	Pliers with wire cutter, three sizes of flathead screwdriver, Phillips screwdriver, square drive, double tooth saw, fine-coarse file, awl, chisel, can/bottle opener, ruler, small blade, and main blade as above. Nylon belt pouch

The SOG Toolclip represents an alternative approach to the multi-tool idea, being built more along the lines of a conventional folding pocket knife. The plier head forms an extension of the handle, with the knife itself providing one handle and the other being hinged out of the back of the knife. The plier head is very square in shape, and incorporates a wire cutter.

Between the stainless steel scales are a drop point main blade, a serrated blade with screwdriver tip and wire-stripping notch, a bottle opener/small utility blade, and a small screwdriver/chisel. The plier handle is held in the closed position by a bail, and may also be used as a light pry bar.

The Toolclip has a spring steel clip attached to one side, so that it may be clipped to pocket or belt

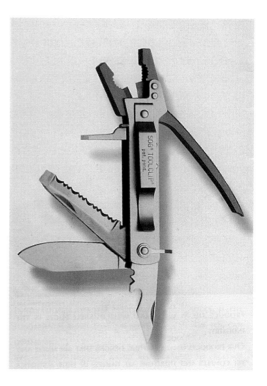

Manufacturer:	SOG Speciality Knives Inc., Edmonds, Washington, USA
Model:	Toolclip
Length overall:	5 1/4in. (closed)
Blade length:	3in.
Blade shape:	Drop point (main blade)
Blade material:	All stainless steel
Edge:	Flat-ground
Grip:	Stainless steel scales, with single plier handle at edge
Construction:	Blades and tools sandwiched between pinned stainless steel scales
Features:	Pliers with wire cutter, utility blade with bottle opener and wire stripper, serrated edge blade with metal file and screwdriver, small screwdriver, pocket/belt clip

The Micro Toolclip takes the theme of the Toolclip, but in a smaller overall size. In addition to the plier/wire-cutter head, there are three blades - a drop point, a serrated edge sheepsfoot, and a file with screwdriver tip and wire-stripper notch. As with the Toolclip, the hinged plier handle may be used as a light duty pry bar.

The Micro Toolclip has polycarbonate scales and is available in a range of colours including black, yellow, green and red. On the back of the handle is a pocket/belt clip.

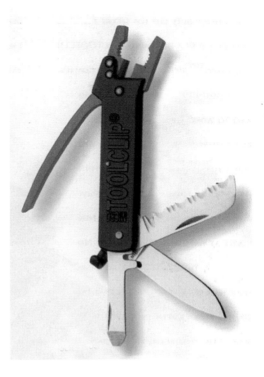

Manufacturer:	Made in Japan for SOG Speciality Knives Inc., Edmonds, Washington, USA
Model:	Micro Toolclip
Length overall:	3 3/4in. (closed)
Blade length:	2in.
Blade shape:	Drop point main blade, sheepsfoot serrated blade
Blade material:	Stainless steel
Edge:	Flat-ground
Grip:	Polycarbonate scales in choice of colours, with single plier handle at edge
Construction:	Blades and tools sandwiched between pinned stainless steel liners and polycarbonate scales
Features:	Pliers with wire cutter, two blades as above, file with screwdriver tip and wire stripper, pocket/belt clip

Before the Leatherman and its imitators came along, there was really only one multi-tool to choose from - the Swiss Army Knife. This distinctive knife, with its red plastic scales and enormous selection of stainless steel tools, has been a favourite of soldiers, boy scouts, campers and outdoorsmen for years and still has much to commend it. A well chosen Swiss Army Knife will tackle just about any light job and is handy for everyday chores as well as invaluable in a survival situation.

It is important to remember, however, that the Swiss Army Knife is essentially a light duty tool and cannot tackle the heavy jobs that are essential in a survival situation, such as shelter building, fire preparation and digging, etc. It is of no use for fighting. The ideal combination for survival would be a Swiss Army Knife or similar multi-tool, carried together with a big knife or machete for chopping, hacking and digging.

The standard Victorinox Swiss Army Knife is 3 1/2in. long and 1in. deep. The width of the knife depends on the number and types of tool in any particular model - further tools are accommodated by adding layers in the sandwich of scale/liner/blade/liner/blade/liner/scale. Shorter and thinner tools are paired within a single blade space - the standard blade and small blade, for instance, sit together between two liners. Larger tools, like the scissors or the pliers, require a space to themselves.

A knife with half a dozen or so tools may still be regarded as a pocket knife, but above this size it becomes too heavy and bulky to slip into a pocket and is best carried in webbing or a belt pouch. Some of the

larger models come with a black leather belt pouch with pockets for additional small items, including a sharpening stone, compass/ruler, pencil, sticking plasters and needle and thread.

Victorinox also produce smaller Swiss Army Knives, measuring 2 1/4in. when closed, with a small main blade, scissors and nail file. There is a larger range, measuring 4 3/8in. closed, which has a locking mechanism for the main blade.

There is not space here to list all the possible combinations of tools available in the many Swiss Army Knives. Instead, as an example, here is a list of the tools and blades found on the Swiss Champ, one of the larger models:

Main blade 2 3/4in. drop point, small blade 1 5/8in. drop point, metal file/saw, woodsaw, fish hook disgorger/descaler, scissors, light pliers/wire cutters, Phillips screwdriver, magnifying glass, bottle opener/medium screwdriver, can opener/small screwdriver, awl/reamer, small screwdriver, light chisel, corkscrew containing separate fine screwdriver, tweezers, ballpoint pen, toothpick, lanyard ring. In the knife's separate leather belt pouch are found: sharpening stone, clutch pencil, ruler/compass, length of fine nylon twine, matches, safety pins, writing paper, sticking plasters, needles and thread. All this fits into a belt pouch which measures 4 1/4in. x 2 1/2in. x 1 3/4in.. Combined with a good sized knife or machete, and with a few minor additions, it would make a sound survival kit in a remarkably compact package.

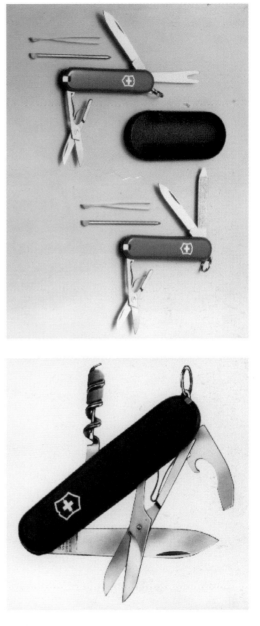

Manufacturer: Victorinox, Switzerland

Model: Swiss Champ

Length overall: 3 1/2in.

Blade length: Main blade 2 3/4in.

Blade shape: Drop point

Blade material: Stainless steel

Edge: Flat-ground

Grip: Red plastic scales with Swiss flag logo

Construction: Blades/tools sandwiched between pinned steel liners

Features: Huge variety of blade/tool options available

The name of Victorinox tends to be associated most firmly with Swiss Army Knives, but Wenger of Switzerland have an equally good claim to be a maker of 'genuine' Swiss Army Knives, and produce a similarly wide range of multi-function knives with red plastic scales.

At first glance the knives are identical, but a closer look reveals vital differences. The first clue is the Swiss cross symbol - on Wenger's knives this is set in a rounded box, instead of the shield seen on the Victorinox knives. Wenger knives also have a short length of chain on the lanyard ring, whereas Victorinox knives do not.

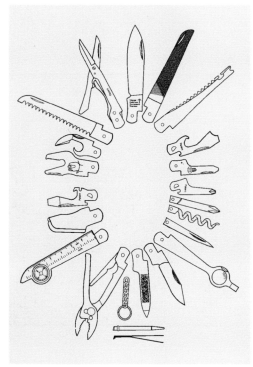

Wenger's tools are very similar to those of Victorinox - the knife blades, reamer, can and bottle openers, for instance, are virtually identical. Other tools, however, show some improvements. The Phillips screwdriver and bottle opener/screwdriver have a patented safety lock mechanism that locks them open when pressure is applied to the tip. This prevents their folding closed at the vital moment when the maximum pressure is applied. The scissors have micro-grooved edges which grip difficult materials like fishing line to give better cutting performance. They also make use of a clever lever system to dispense with the vulnerable flat steel spring, using instead the spring in the knife back to return them to the open position when the pressure is released. This system is also employed on the pliers, which have a slot so the gape may be extended to tackle larger items.

Wenger knives tend not to be so widely marketed as Victorinox, at least in the UK, but if one is planning to buy a Swiss Army Knife it is well worth looking for them, in case the slight differences in the tools appear preferable.

Manufacturer:	Wenger, Switzerland
Model:	Supertalent
Length overall:	3 1/2in.
Blade length:	Main blade 2 3/4in.
Blade shape:	Drop point
Blade material:	Stainless steel
Edge:	Flat-ground
Grip:	Red plastic scales with Swiss flag logo
Construction:	Blades/tools sandwiched between pinned steel liners
Features:	Huge variety of blade/tool options available

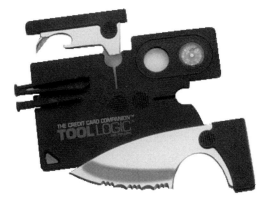

Manufacturer:	ToolLogic Inc.
Model:	Credit Card Companion
Length overall:	3 3/8in. x 2 1/8in. x 3/16in.
Blade length:	1 7/8in.
Blade shape:	Drop point
Blade material:	Stainless steel
Edge:	Serrated
Grip:	Truncated, square-ended grip with deep finger groove
Construction:	Credit-card sized unit incorporates compass and lens, with pull-out blade and small tools
Features:	Compass, x8 magnifying lens, can/bottle opener, awl, tweezers, toothpick, screwdriver

The ToolLogic Credit Card Companion is an extraordinarily light and compact item that manages to cram a useful knife blade plus a surprising number of tools into a package little bigger than a credit card.

The whole thing is just 3/16in. thick, and measures the same as a credit card - 3 3/8in. x 2 1/8in.. The case is made of black Zytel, and incorporates a compass, x8 magnifying lens and lanyard hole. Separate tweezers and a toothpick are located in holes in the card, and can be pulled out with a fingernail.

At the top of the card is housed a combined can/ bottle opener and screwdriver. The main part of the card forms the sheath for a knife with a 1 7/8in. serrated drop point blade. The restricted size of the knife means that it does not have a conventional handle. Instead the handle is cut off square and there is a deep finger groove which enables the knife to be held firmly between thumb and first finger. Alternative holds are possible - the knife may be inverted for cutting upwards, or held in the manner of a push-dagger. The shortened tang is covered with black Zytel, to match the card and to provide a better grip.

This knife is too small for anything but very light work, and would not provide a serious alternative to a conventional knife. However, it is small and unobtrusive enough to be carried anywhere, and in an emergency with nothing else available it would be invaluable.

United Cutlery's Utili Tool is one of several credit-card sized survival/utility tools which consist of a flat piece of steel with sharpened edges, points and cut-outs to tackle a range of light jobs such as cutting, piercing and removing bottle tops.

This one has its own slim case of black ABS plastic to protect it when carried in a wallet or pocket.

Its functions include: can opener, knife edge, screwdriver, bottle opener, wrench, magnifying lens and ruler.

As with the ToolLogic Card, the Utili Tool is too small to be useful for anything but the lightest jobs, and is no alternative to a knife - but unlike a knife it can be carried anywhere and provides the ability to tackle a number of jobs that would otherwise be impossible in an emergency.

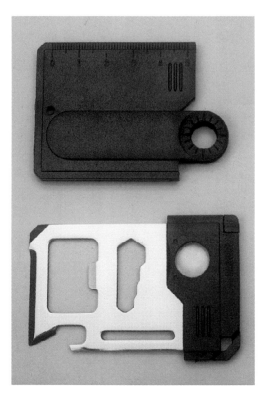

Manufacturer:	Made in Taiwan for United Cutlery, Sevierville, Tennessee, USA
Model:	Utili Tool
Length overall:	3 1/8in. x 2in.
Blade length:	1 3/4in.
Blade shape:	Sharpened straight edge of rectangular piece of steel
Blade material:	420J2 stainless steel
Edge:	Bevel-ground
Grip:	ABS plastic cover on one end of steel rectangle
Construction:	Plastic grip moulded on to steel
Features:	See text

FOLDING KNIVES

Manufacturer: Al Mar Knives Inc., Lake Oswego, Oregon, USA

Model: SERE Attack Models I and II

Length overall: SERE Attack II 6in. closed, SERE Attack I 5in. closed

Blade length: SERE Attack II 4in., SERE Attack I 3in.

Blade shape: Spear point

Blade material: Stainless steel, Rc 57-59

Edge: Bevel-ground with false top edge

Grip: Green micarta or neoprene; brushed stainless bolster; lanyard hole

Construction: Scales pinned through liners; blade swivels on hinge pin; springback lock mechanism

Features: Black leather belt sheath

Like Al Mar's fixed-blade SERE knives, the folding models - the SERE Attack I and II - were conceived by Col. Nick Rowe, a Special Operations Commando based at Fort Bragg in North Carolina. The initials SERE stand for Survival, Escape, Resistance, Evasion and those are exactly the situations these strong little folders are intended for.

The Attack II is the bigger of the two, with an overall length of 6in. when closed, and a blade length of 4in.. The blade has a spear point, with a false back edge for half its length, and the main edge is bevel-ground. There is a thumbnail slot for opening. It is a sturdy blade which gives good penetration and cutting performance.

The handle has inner brass liners, with stainless steel bolsters, spine and locking mechanism. The grip is contoured neoprene or green micarta, with longitudinal grooves, and an inset square brass medallion featuring the Al Mar logo. The bolster on the left hand side has a 'special forces' logo of crossed arrows and a sword. There is a tubular steel rivet at the butt which forms a lanyard hole.

The Attack I is similar, but slightly smaller, at 5in. overall, with a 3in. blade.

Either knife would make a useful field tool, although neither has the length or weight for chopping and is too small to be a serious fighter - although well capable of serving the purpose if the occasion demands. For other general tasks, though, these knives are an excellent choice.

The Applegate Combat Folder was developed by Col. Rex Applegate from the Applegate-Fairbairn fixed blade fighting knife, to provide an effective fighter which can be carried discreetly in a pocket or a small pouch or sheath.

The knife shares a number of features with its fixed-blade cousin, as well as having the same look and feel. The blade is very similar, with a spear pointed dagger shape, and the basic shape of the grip is close to that of the original A-F Fighter. Obviously some changes were necessary to turn the fixed blade model into a folder - the wide double guard of the A-F has gone, and in its place is a waisted section on the handle to keep fingers off the blade. The blade itself, at 4 1/2in., is considerably smaller than the 6 1/2in. of the A-F Fighter - after all, it has to fold away into the handle - but Applegate has managed to fit a surprisingly large blade snugly into a comfortably shaped handle.

The blade shape is designed to provide excellent penetration and stabbing performance, with a diamond-shaped cross-section for strength since a knife blade may break surprisingly easily when used for stabbing, either through striking bone or through the massive sideways forces exerted as the muscles go into spasm. The knife's blade is also effective for slashing: the serrated section on the main edge helps to rip through clothing etc. and create a deep, debilitating wound. The blade is not big and heavy enough for hacking and chopping, however.

The blade has a thumb stud so that it can be deployed quickly and surely with one hand - allowing the user to keep one hand free, either for defence as the knife is deployed, or to keep hold of another weapon. Once the blade is opened, it locks firmly in place by means of a liner lock mechanism. This is preferable to a springback in a fighting folder, since it is stronger and less likely to be released inadvertently by the hand holding the handle.

The handle is similar to that of the A-F Fighter, made of glass-filled nylon and contoured to fit the hand, with longitudinal grooves for extra grip. The finger/thumb grooves are ridged to reduce the chance of the hand slipping on to the blade.

This knife is unusual in being designed primarily as a fighter - most folding knives are basically general-purpose blades, although some have features intended to make them more suitable for fighting. Although the Applegate Combat Folder excels at its intended purpose, it is also versatile enough to make a handy general purpose blade which could be used for a multitude of everyday tasks.

Manufacturer:	Gerber (a division of Fiskars Inc.), Portland, Oregon, USA
Model:	Applegate Combat Folder
Length overall:	5 3/4in. closed, 10 1/4in. open
Blade length:	4 1/2in.
Blade shape:	Spear point dagger
Blade material:	425 modified stainless steel, 57 Rc
Edge:	Bevel-ground, with serrated section
Grip:	Contoured glass-filled nylon handle with longitudinal grooves
Construction:	Blade swivels on hinge pin; grip scales on liners, with locking mechanism
Features:	Thumb stud for easy deployment of blade

Designed in conjunction with Chris Caracci, a former US Navy SEAL, Benchmade's AFCK - or Advanced Folding Combat Knife - is a strong and handy general purpose blade. Although not primarily designed as a fighter, it is nevertheless up to that job if the occasion demands.

The knife has a 3 9/10in. blade of ATS-34 stainless steel, with a Rockwell hardness of 59-61, and a satin finish. The main edge is convex, with an aggressive, serrated section near the handle. There is an extended straight clip with a false edge, giving a very sharp point which is excellent for penetration and for fine work.

The blade has a thumb hole so that it can be opened quickly and easily with either hand. This is the same as the Spyderco system and is licensed by that company for use in this knife. The blade locks with a titanium liner-lock mechanism, which provides a strong lock-up which is not easily released accidentally when the knife is in use - a knurled section of the liner must be pushed sideways with the thumb to release the lock.

The handle is made of bead blasted G-10 laminate, with a chequered surface for grip. It is a slim, contoured handle with a deep finger groove, which gives a good firm hold. The finger groove is set back from the hilt, effectively increasing the blade length but still allowing the grip to be choked up for fine work. A stainless steel clip allows the knife to be clipped to a belt or pocket. The handle has an inset medallion with Benchmade's butterfly logo and there is a lanyard hole.

The knife is also available with the blade finished in a proprietary Black-T finish which is highly resistant to salt water corrosion. A Mini AFCK is also available, with an overall length of 7in. (open) and a blade length of 3 1/4in..

Manufacturer:	Benchmade Knife Co Inc., Clackamas, Oregon, USA
Model:	AFCK - Advanced Folding Combat Knife
Length overall:	9in. open, 5.7/10in. closed
Blade length:	3.9/10in.
Blade shape:	Clip point with opening hole
Blade material:	ATS-34 stainless steel, satin finish, Rc 59-61
Edge:	Bevel-ground with false back edge and serrated section near grip
Grip:	Black chequered G-10 laminate scales, with bead blasted finish; deep index finger groove
Construction:	Scales fitted to 6AL-4V titanium liners; inset medallion with butterfly trademark
Features:	Easy opening Spyderco type thumb hole; liner locking mechanism; belt/pocket clip

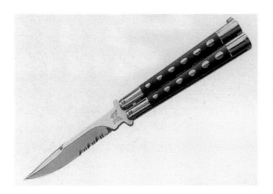

Manufacturer:	Benchmade Knife Co Inc., Clackamas, Oregon, USA
Model:	Bali-Song range
Length overall:	9 1/4in. open, 5 1/4in. closed
Blade length:	4in.
Blade shape:	Large range available, including several clip point and drop point designs
Blade material:	Stainless steel
Edge:	Range includes flat- and bevel-grind, types, with and without serrations
Grip:	Several styles available, including die-cast skeleton designs
Construction:	Two-part handle hinged at ricasso, folds out to expose blade
Features:	Illegal in UK

The 'Butterfly' knife or Bali-Song has become notorious as a favoured weapon of criminals and is banned in the UK and certain other countries. It is unfortunate that misuse has led to this type of knife being unavailable to many legitimate users, since it is a good practical design which is equally effective for legitimate purposes.

The basic principle of the Bali-Song is that the handle is formed of two parts, hinged separately at the blade. With the knife closed, the blade is completely enclosed by the handles, which are held together by a clip at the butt end. To open the knife, one unlatches the clip and swings the handles in opposite directions through 180˚, so that they come together and can be clipped together with the latch. This provides a knife almost as rigid as a fixed blade, with no possibility of the blade's folding shut in use; yet when closed the blade is totally enclosed and completely safe. The system is one of the few folding designs that allows a double-edged blade to be used without risk of injury when the knife is folded.

Benchmade produce a wide range of Bali-Song knives, with an enormous variety of blades including clip points, drop points, spear points, chisel points, and a 'weehawk' blade - a type of spear/clip blade which combines tip strength with good penetration. Blades are of stainless steel, with Zamak die-cast handles, some with black or wood inserts. Blade lengths are generally 3in. or 4in., with overall lengths of 7 1/2in. or 9 1/4in. when open, 4 3/8in. or 5 1/4in. closed.

The CQC7, or 970, was designed by Ernest Emerson as a tough, lightweight, folding combat knife. Since its introduction it has become Benchmade's most popular folding tactical knife and with good reason. The 970 is an immensely strong and rugged knife which offers excellent performance in a convenient and lightweight package.

The knife measures 4 5/8in. long when closed, and has a 3 3/8in. blade with a thumb stud for one-handed opening. The blade is a clipped chisel point design, ground on one side only for added strength. It is made of 1/8in. thick ATS-34 stainless steel, hardened to Rc 59-61, with a bead-blasted finish. It has a serrated section near the handle on the main edge and there is a raised and grooved thumb section on the back of the blade, allowing one to exert a powerful downward pressure for cutting and penetrating.

The handle is formed of titanium liners with flat bead-blasted G-10 laminate scales, chequered for extra grip. The right-hand liner is sprung to form a strong liner lock to keep the blade firmly in the open position until the lock is released.

The 970 is an extremely rugged and versatile knife which will tackle a multitude of general chores and may also be used for fighting - although any folder is very much a last resort to be used when other weapons are unavailable.

Variations on the 970 include a pocket clip version, a long-bladed model with 3.95in. blade, and an 'automatic' model which utilises a coil spring to deploy the blade simply by pressing a release button in the handle (this latter model is subject to legal restrictions in many countries).

Manufacturer:	Benchmade Knife Co Inc., Clackamas, Oregon, USA
Model:	970
Length overall:	8in. (open), 4 5/8in. (closed)
Blade length:	3 3/8in.
Blade shape:	Clipped chisel point
Blade material:	ATS-34 stainless steel, bead blasted finish, Rc 59-61
Edge:	Bevel-ground one side only, with serrated section near grip
Grip:	Black chequered G-10 laminate scales, with bead blasted finish
Construction:	Scales fitted to 6AL-4V titanium liners
Features:	Easy opening thumb stud; liner locking mechanism

Britain and other NATO armies issue a simple, rugged, stainless-steel folding utility knife which incorporates a main blade and a small selection of tools. The main blade is 2 1/2in. long, of a flat-ground sheepsfoot design. This is good for simple cutting jobs, but is not suitable for fine point work, piercing or chopping, etc.

Typical models also include a can/bottle opener blade, and there is often a thick marlin spike hinged at the back of the knife.

Construction is simple, with the blades sandwiched between pinned stainless steel scales; a stainless steel spring snaps the blades into the open position but does not lock them. One scale is extended to form a screwdriver blade, and there is a bail which may be used to attach a lanyard.

The knife is immensely strong and corrosion resistant, but is not particularly comfortable to use owing to the lack of contoured grip scales.

Manufacturer:	Ministry of Defence contractors, UK
Model:	Folding Knife
Length overall:	3 11/16in. closed, 6 1/2in. with main blade open
Blade length:	2 1/2in.
Blade shape:	Sheepsfoot main blade
Blade material:	Stainless steel
Edge:	Flat-ground
Grip:	Stainless steel scales
Construction:	All stainless steel, pinned through scales
Features:	Marlin spike, can/bottle opener, lanyard bail

Made in France, Opinel knives are of a long-established design admired for its simplicity. There is a range of sizes, from the tiny 2 1/4in. model up to the 6 1/4in. model 12, but the most popular are the models 6 and 8, with closed lengths of 3 3/4in. and 4 1/4in., respectively.

The design is basic, with a simple drop point blade hinged in a turned wooden handle. The blades are of carbon steel, although the models 6 and 8 are also available in stainless steel. The bolster is strengthened with a steel collar and there is an outer collar which is turned to lock the blade in position. The blade features Opinel's 'crowned hand' logo.

The blade may often be stiff to open - especially since the wooden handle shrinks and swells depending on atmospheric temperature and humidity - and owners soon get into the habit of giving the butt of the knife a smart tap on a hard surface to free the blade and partly open it, rather than risk a broken fingernail by using the notch.

Although this somewhat dated design has considerable drawbacks, it has a loyal following of users who are looking for a simple, reliable knife. As a general purpose folder it has a certain appeal, with the advantage that being inexpensive it can be treated as disposable.

Manufacturer:	Opinel, France
Model:	Dimensions below are for Model 8
Length overall:	4 1/4in. closed
Blade length:	3 1/8in.
Blade shape:	Drop point
Blade material:	Carbon steel (stainless version available)
Edge:	Flat-ground
Grip:	Contoured rounded wooden handle
Construction:	Blade hinged on pin through handle, strengthened at joint with steel collar and locking collar
Features:	Range of sizes available; also specialist blades including pruning saw and hooked pruning blade

Designed for wartime parachutists, this unusual knife has the advantage that it is effectively a fixed-blade knife when opened, but folds down so that the blade is totally enclosed in the handle and cannot cause injury.

It is an ingenious design, using two handle halves hinged at the bolster and connected to the base of the blade by hinged linkages. To open the knife and extend the blade, one first releases a clip that holds the two handle pieces together. The handles are then pulled apart at the middle, so that the linkages begin to pull the blade out through the slot in the bolster. The base of the blade must be pushed past the centre position, after which the handles can be squeezed together to push the blade fully out. With the hand holding the handles, the blade cannot then retract into the handle again, and by reclosing the clip the knife effectively becomes a fixed blade.

The blade is a spear point design, made of 420 J2 stainless steel, and measures 5 1/4in. long. When folded, the knife is 6 7/8in. long.

This type of knife is banned from sale in the UK, although one suspects this is largely due to the fact that its design is easy to define in law; it is no more dangerous or prone to misuse than a simple butcher's knife and it has considerable safety advantages for legitimate users.

This knife is more than just a gimmick. It is a useful all-round field tool, although a little too light and small to be good for heavy chopping work. The all-steel construction makes it unsuitable for use in extreme cold without some form of protection for the hands.

Manufacturer:	Distributed by United Cutlery, Sevierville, Tennessee, USA
Model:	Paratrooper
Length overall:	6 7/8in. (closed); small version 5in., with clip point blade
Blade length:	5 1/4in.
Blade shape:	Spear point
Blade material:	420 J2 stainless steel
Edge:	Bevel-ground
Grip:	Pentograph design hinged at guard allows blade to be retracted into handle by swinging handle halves outwards
Construction:	Folded sheet steel handles with steel pin hinges
Features:	Safety latch holds knife in open or closed position. Illegal in UK

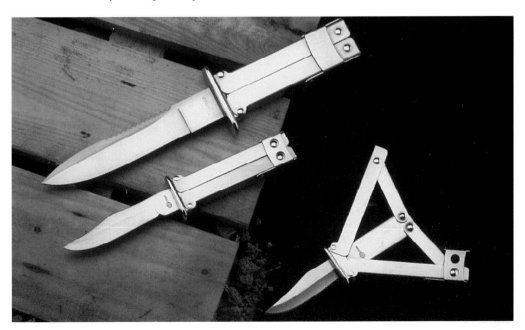

Designed by Blackie Collins, the Smith & Wesson First Response knife is intended to be carried by paramedics, traffic police and others who may be first on an accident scene and need to free trapped casualties.

It has a spring-loaded glass-breaker punch tool built into the handle. This is cocked by pulling a tab back against spring pressure and folding it over to engage in a slot. To break a vehicle or aircraft window, the butt of the knife is held against the glass, and the tab pushed out of engagement, releasing a pointed punch which smashes into the glass with considerable force, causing it to crack - something which is remarkably hard to do without a heavy implement.

The knife blade has a serrated edge which is good for cutting through seat belts, rope, etc. It has a screwdriver tip which can be used for prying window seals, for instance.

This is a special purpose knife which excels at rescue work, but is severely limited by its specialist design for more general tasks.

Manufacturer:	Smith & Wesson, Springfield, MA, USA
Model:	First Response
Length overall:	4 1/2in. closed
Blade length:	3 3/4in.
Blade shape:	Slightly convex edge with screwdriver tip
Blade material:	440 stainless steel
Edge:	Bevel-ground
Grip:	Moulded black Zytel with chequered panels
Construction:	Liner lock mechanism
Features:	Spring-loaded glass-breaker tool in handle.
	Black Cordura sheath with boot/belt clip

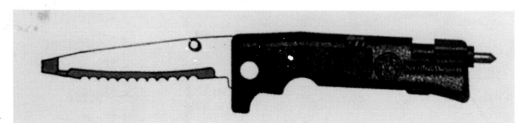

The SOG Tomcat is a modern, high-tech folding knife which makes use of stainless steel and Kraton for high performance. It is a relatively small but sturdy knife, with a 3 3/4in. blade of 1/5in. thick 440C stainless steel. The blade is a double clip design, derived from SOG's fixed-blade knives such as the Trident. It is very strong for its size, with excellent penetration and good cutting performance.

The handle is chequered black Kraton rubber, with stainless steel bolsters, and there is a lockback mechanism to hold the blade open in use.

This is a solid little knife, well suited to a range of tasks, and strong enough to be used as a last resort fighter.

Based on the Tomcat are SOG's Stingray and Sogwinder folding knives, which offer different blade shapes and sizes in a similar design.

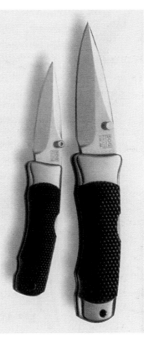

Manufacturer:	SOG Knives, Edmonds, Washington, USA
Model:	Tomcat
Length overall:	8 1/4in. open
Blade length:	3 3/4in.
Blade shape:	Double clip Bowie
Blade material:	1/5in. thick 440-C stainless steel, Rc 57-58
Edge:	Bevel-ground, with false double clip edge
Grip:	Chequered Kraton scales
Construction:	Induction welded bolsters
Features:	All stainless steel construction. Dual mounting nylon scabbard

The SPF50 Marine Combat is a lockback folder based on the US Marine Corps combat knife. Like that knife, it has a clipped Bowie-style blade; the fuller of the USMC knife is retained to provide a thumb notch, which allows one-handed opening. The folder's blade measures approximately 4in., and has a serrated section for about half the length of the main edge.

Like many of the Spec Plus fixed-blade knives, the SPF50 has a 1095 carbon steel blade with a black epoxy powder coating to minimise shine and protect the blade from corrosion.

The handle is similar to those of Spec Plus fixed-blade knives also. Made of 'Gnvory' - a reinforced nylon material - it is black in colour and has deep lateral grooves for added grip. The handle incorporates a lanyard hole, and there is a thumb-operated lockback mechanism to lock the blade open when in use.

The SPF51 Navy Survival and SPF52 Jump are similar knives, but with different blade shapes derived from well established military service patterns.

Marine Combat.

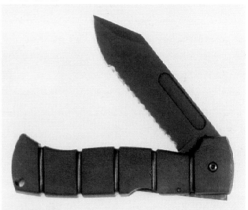

Navy Survival.

Jump.

Manufacturer:	Ontario Knife Co., Franklinville, New York, USA
Model:	SPF50 Marine Combat
Length overall:	5 1/4in. (closed)
Blade length:	4in.
Blade shape:	Bowie-style clip point
Blade material:	1095 carbon steel with epoxy powder coated black finish
Edge:	Bevel ground, part serrated
Grip:	Black Gnvory grooved handle
Construction:	Springback-type locking mechanism
Features:	Leather and Cordura belt sheath

Spyderco's Military folder is a development of their popular Police Model, designed to offer more heft but with little extra weight. It measures 5 1/4in. overall, with a 4in. blade of high performance CPM 440V steel. The blade is typical Spyderco - a convex main edge, with a straight back rising to incorporate a thumb hole for easy one-handed opening. The hole is larger than usual, at 9/16in., so that it may be used with a gloved hand.

Just behind this hole is a ridged portion which the thumb falls naturally into for extra cutting power. The blade is available with a plain edge or with Spyderco's SpyderEdge serrations, renowned for their ability to slice through difficult materials such as webbing or rope.

The handle is made from Spauldite G-10 epoxy filled glass composite, and is contoured to fit the hand well. It has a clip on the right-hand side, which may be used to clip the knife on belt, boot or pocket. Inside is a Walker Linerlock, which holds the blade firmly when in use, but which may be readily released by pushing the knurled section inwards with the thumb.

This is a high performance folder from a company with a strong reputation among service personnel. It is available with a black non-reflective finish to blade, lock, clip and pivot pin.

Manufacturer:	Spyderco Inc., Goldon, Colorado, USA
Model:	C36 Military
Length overall:	5 1/4in.
Blade length:	4in.
Blade shape:	Straight back convex edge, with 9/16in. thumb hole at rear of top edge
Blade material:	CPM 440V steel, black titanium finish available
Edge:	Flat-ground; plain or serrated edge versions available
Grip:	Spauldite G-10 scales
Construction:	Walker liner lock mechanism
Features:	Pocket/belt clip

Timberline's Timberlite range has proved popular with service and civilian users due to the knives' light yet strong and rugged design. The Police range offers two sizes of knife - 4in. and 4 1/2in. when closed - with a strong spear point blade.

The blade has a convex main edge, with a high performance serrated section near the handle. The main edge is ground with a slight hollow. A false back edge is then ground to provide what is effectively a spear point, giving a tip that is strong but penetrates well and is fine enough for delicate work.

The blade has a plastic thumb stud which enables it to be opened one-handedly with either hand. Locking is by a patented Neeley Lock mechanism. This is an unusual but effective system in which the pivot pin sits in a slot in the blade, rather than the usual round hole. As the blade comes into the fully open position, a spring pulls the blade back into the handle, engaging it into a shaped recess in the handle. The blade is then firmly locked open until the blade is pulled directly away from the handle in the direction of the tip; any pressure on the tip or edge of the blade simply locks it more firmly.

The handle is a single piece moulded from Zytel, with chequered panels for grip.

There is a belt/pocket clip, also made from Zytel, on the right-hand side. The knife is available with a polished or matte stainless finish, or black titanium coating.

Manufacturer:	Timberline, USA
Model:	Police Model Folder
Length overall:	4 1/2in.
Blade length:	3 1/8in.
Blade shape:	Spear point
Blade material:	425 stainless steel, Rc 58, black titanium finish available
Edge:	Hollow-ground main edge with serrated section, false back edge
Grip:	Chequered, black reinforced nylon
Construction:	One-piece moulded handle, patented Neeley lock mechanism
Features:	Thumb stud on blade for easy opening. Belt/pocket clip on handle

UTILITY AND
SPECIAL PURPOSE BLADES

The Cobra is intended as a multi-purpose survival tool, capable of the various heavy tasks required by the survivor in a hostile environment. The unusual blade shape can be used to clear vegetation, chop and split wood for a raft, fire or shelter, dig, gut and butcher large animals, hammer nails, and much more besides. Advertisements for the Cobra claim that it will cut all the requirements for a raft, and then be used as a paddle.

The unique curve of the blade provides different types of edge for specific tasks. The hooked curve near the tip is good for clearing light vegetation, as it catches the stems and then cuts them as it is dragged through. The tip itself is sharply pointed, unlike the more traditional machete-shaped blades and so may be used for quite delicate piercing jobs - opening a carcass, for instance. Used in conjunction with the hook, this is particularly useful for gutting fish and animals.

For heavier duty chopping and splitting tasks, the deep bellied curve comes into its own. The sheer weight of the blade allows a powerful chopping stroke, and the convex-belly edge provides a reverse curve that cuts particularly well.

The story goes that the knife's designer discovered by accident that the Cobra also works as a decoy - when chopped into a fencepost at an upright angle, it has a silhouette similar to that of a crow or hawk and will attract other birds.

Manufacturer:	Bay Knife Co., USA. Distributed in the UK by Resource Services, Bracknell, Berkshire
Model:	Cobra
Length overall:	16in.
Blade length:	11in.
Blade shape:	Deep-bellied, hook-ended machete-style blade
Blade material:	Carbon steel, Rc 48-55, Teflon coated
Edge:	Bevel-ground
Grip:	Black composite with guard and lanyard hole
Construction:	Handle pinned to full-length tang
Features:	Multi-purpose survival tool

The name and appearance of the Cold Steel Special Projects Bad Axe suggest that it was intended more as a weapon than a tool, although it is difficult to imagine many soldiers choosing to carry such a weapon in preference to a more versatile tool, or even a few extra rounds of ammunition.

The double-edged bat-wing style head is equally effective at chopping in either direction, which would make this a fearsome weapon in close quarter combat. The flat steel blades have ridges to provide extra strength and resist any tendency for them to fold over in heavy use.

However, as a survival tool its uses are limited: it would no doubt be handy for shelter building and clearing undergrowth and could be used as a paddle, but it would be unsuitable for digging or food preparation.

Manufacturer:	Special Projects Division, Cold Steel Inc., Ventura, California, USA
Model:	92BX Bad Axe
Length overall:	20in.
Blade length:	7 1/4in. edge length x 8 1/8in. width
Blade shape:	Butterfly-shaped double-sided axe
Blade material:	Carbon steel with black finish
Edge:	Bevel-ground
Grip:	Straight round-section hardwood handle
Construction:	Handle pinned into hollow tubular section of head
Features:	Strengthening ridges in blade flats

The Gurkha kukri, with its heavy, downward-curved, forward-weighted blade, has earned a reputation as a wickedly effective combat weapon as well as a versatile survival tool. This Special Projects version from Cold Steel offers all the advantages of the traditional kukri blade, but in a purely practical stylised form which omits features such as the blade notch, and takes advantage of modern materials including Kraton and Cordura.

The Special Projects kukri has a high carbon blade of 1/8in. thick steel - somewhat thinner than that of the Gurkha kukri. It has a deeper belly than the traditional shape, however, which goes some way towards making up the weight lost in the thickness. Like the traditional kukri, the Special Projects version has most of its weight in the forward portion of the blade, allowing a powerful chopping stroke.

The reverse curve of the edge provides phenomenal cutting performance.

The handle is softer and more rounded than in the Gurkha version, making it more comfortable for extended heavy use, such as constructing a raft or shelter. The black finish on the blade cuts down reflections, as well as helping to protect the steel from the elements.

Manufacturer:	Special Projects Division, Cold Steel Inc., Ventura, California, USA
Model:	35LTC Kukri
Length overall:	17in.
Blade length:	12in.
Blade shape:	Kukri (traditional notch omitted)
Blade material:	1/8in. thick, high carbon steel, black epoxy powder coated
Edge:	Bevel-ground
Grip:	Chequered and contoured one-piece, black Kraton rubber handle with flared butt and lanyard hole
Construction:	Kraton handle moulded to full-length tang
Sheath:	Black Cordura belt sheath

During the Cold War, legend had it that the elite Soviet *Spetsnaz* forces trained in the use of several exotic weapons, including a special entrenching shovel with sharpened edges which could be swung like a battle axe or thrown at an enemy. No doubt there was an element of truth in this, but suggestions that *Spetsnaz* troops would use their shovels to eliminate sentries from a distance sound like pure propaganda.

The Cold Steel Special Projects Special Forces Shovel is modelled after the original *Spetsnaz* version and is a relatively crude but effective tool with a multitude of uses.

Every soldier needs a shovel or entrenching tool, and the design of this one allows it to be used as a paddle, hammer, hatchet and battle axe as well as for the more mundane tasks of digging trenches and latrines. It is relatively light to carry, at 28.6oz, but still solid enough to be useful as a weapon and multi-purpose field tool. For survival purposes it would be best carried along with a good knife.

Manufacturer:	Special Projects Division, Cold Steel Inc., Ventura, California, USA
Model:	92SF Special Forces Shovel
Length overall:	20 1/2in.
Blade length:	7 1/2in.
Blade shape:	Shovel with sharpened edges
Blade material:	Carbon steel with black finish
Edge:	Bevel-ground
Grip:	Straight round-section hardwood handle
Construction:	Handle pinned into hollow tubular section of head
Features:	Modelled on Soviet *Spetsnaz* shovel, intended for multiple uses including digging, paddling, hammering, chopping, throwing and close quarter combat

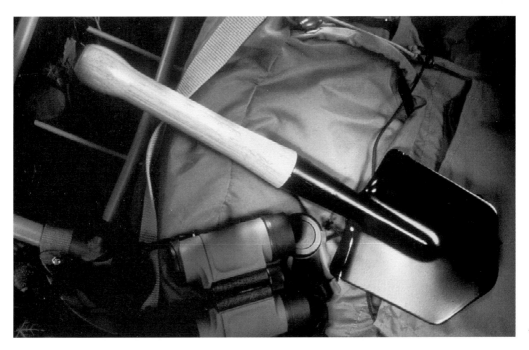

Knife throwing may look good in the cinema, but there is little call for it in real life battle, or for that matter in special operations. Nevertheless, Cold Steel have produced their True Flight Thrower for those who wish to practise the art.

The knife is 10 3/4in. overall, and consists of a single flat piece of steel, with a simple cord wrap for a handle. The balance is designed to be suitable for throwing, with the moment of inertia well forward, and the steel used is a relatively soft high carbon type to resist any tendency to chip on striking a hard surface at speed.

Unlike some specialist throwing knives, the blade is a conventional drop point shape, making this knife also suitable as a general purpose tool.

Manufacturer:	Special Projects Division, Cold Steel Inc., Ventura, California, USA
Model:	80TFT True Flight Thrower
Length overall:	10 3/4in.
Blade length:	6 1/2in.
Blade shape:	Drop point
Blade material:	High carbon steel, black finished
Edge:	Bevel-ground
Grip:	Cord wrapped around metal tang; lanyard hole
Construction:	One-piece steel, with simple cord-wrap for handle
Sheath:	No sheath

The Cold Steel Special Projects Tomahawk is a modern replica of a weapon which was favoured by certain troops in Vietnam for close quarter combat. The main blade is an effective chopping hatchet type, with a partially sharpened lower edge for hooking. The reverse side provides a fiendish spike which has tremendous penetrating ability and is capable of penetrating a steel helmet and still inflicting a lethal wound to the skull.

The Tomahawk weighs approximately 1lb, with a straight-grain, hickory shaft which effectively extends the user's reach by a foot or so. Although very much a weapon of last resort, it can be lethally effective even in untrained hands. It may be swung at an enemy like a hammer or thrown.

Manufacturer:	Special Projects Division, Cold Steel Inc., Ventura, California, USA
Model:	90VT Vietnam Tomahawk
Length overall:	13 1/2in.
Blade length:	6 1/2in., with 2 3/4in. cutting edge
Blade shape:	Tomahawk shape blade, with spike on reverse edge
Blade material:	Carbon steel, black finished
Edge:	Bevel-ground
Grip:	Straight grain, hickory handle
Construction:	Handle passes through hole in head and is secured by a wedge driven into top of shaft
Sheath:	Oxblood-stained leather sheath to cover head only

Like the Vietnam Tomahawk, the Rifleman's Hawk is a close-quarter combat weapon with a straight shaft and axe-type head. This weapon is around double the weight of the Vietnam version, at 2lb, and is 6in. longer overall.

The hawk head is forged from a single piece of medium carbon 5150 steel, and has a 3 1/2in. cutting edge, with a hammer-head butt.

The weapon may be swung in the hand or thrown at an enemy several yards away. However, throwing is not recommended unless you are confident of hitting the target - otherwise you simply disarm yourself and hand your enemy the means to retaliate!

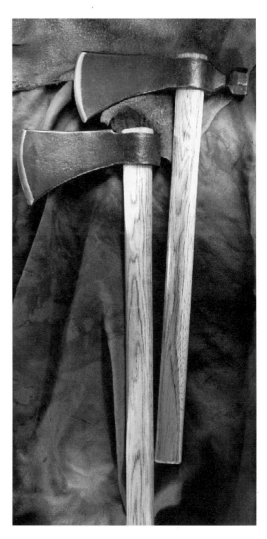

Manufacturer: Special Projects Division, Cold Steel Inc.,
Ventura, California, USA

Model: 90RH Rifleman's Hawk

Length overall: 19 1/2in.

Blade length: 8 1/8in., with 3 1/2in. cutting edge

Blade shape: Tomahawk-shape blade, with hammer head on reverse edge

Blade material: Medium carbon 5150 steel, black finished

Edge: Bevel-ground

Grip: Straight-grain, hickory handle

Construction: Head forged from single piece of steel. Handle passes through hole in head and is secured with wedge driven into top of shaft

Sheath: Oxblood-stained leather sheath to cover head only

The Assegai was a short spear used by Zulu warriors in southern Africa. In the absence of firearms, it revolutionised tribal warfare.

This type of weapon has little relevance in modern warfare, but Cold Steel Special Projects have nevertheless produced this modern version, using a black finished carbon steel blade and American ash handle.

The narrow leaf-shaped spear point blade is sharpened along the full length of its 13 1/2in. double edge, and is effective for both stabbing and slashing - the shaft allowing a single- or double-handed hold.

Manufacturer:	Special Projects Division, Cold Steel Inc., Ventura, California, USA
Model:	95F Assegai
Length overall:	37 1/2in.
Blade length:	13 1/2in.
Blade shape:	Spear
Blade material:	Carbon steel, black finished
Edge:	Bevel-ground
Grip:	Straight ash handle
Construction:	Handle pinned into hollow tubular section of head

The LL 80 is a parachutist's knife developed in 1980 by A. Eickhorn GmbH. It has been developed and improved over the years. Its primary use is for a parachutist to cut himself free if his parachute cords become entangled in a tree, fence or other obstacle. The knife is designed so that the blade falls out under gravity when the lock is operated and the knife held upside-down. This means that the knife may be used one-handedly in an emergency.

As an additional safety feature, the mechanism allows the blade to slide freely back into the handle if there is pressure on the tip. This prevents the parachutist from stabbing himself inadvertently. It also makes the blade virtually useless for self-defence, but there is a fold-out awl at the other end of the handle which may be used for this purpose. The handle also incorporates a bottle opener.

The LL 80 is designed to be disassembled and reassembled without the need for tools, to facilitate cleaning. It will work in any weather conditions, and resists pressure and impacts even up to being run over by a vehicle.

The LL 80 has also proved useful to special forces, police units, tank and aircraft crews.

Manufacturer:	Eickhorn GmbH, Solingen, Germany
Model:	LL 80
Length overall:	
Blade length:	
Blade shape:	Drop point
Blade material:	Stainless steel
Edge:	Flat-ground
Grip:	Green plastic
Construction:	Gravity-operated blade stored in handle, with lock mechanism
Features:	Awl, bottle opener, lanyard bail

The Golok has been a standard British Army issue item for jungle operations for some years and has proved its worth many times over. A basic but effective piece of kit, it consists of a simple flat steel blade with wooden handle. The slight belly to the blade has two functions: the curve improves the cutting performance, and places the weight of the blade well forward. The Golok balances about 4in. in front of the handle, producing a powerful chopping stroke.

The Golok is effective for clearing undergrowth, and performs well at chopping fair sized branches. It may also be used for splitting - preferably by jamming the blade in the grain and then driving it down by hammering with a short section of thick branch. When necessary it can also be pressed into service as a digging tool and pry-bar.

The blade is made of relatively soft carbon steel. This reduces its tendency to chip and makes it easy to sharpen, but it does mean that the Golok loses its edge quite quickly and needs regular sharpening.

The wooden handle is not very forgiving on the hands, and many users bind the handle with cord or twine to give a better grip. For extended periods of use, gloves are advisable.

Manufacturer:	R. Martindale & Co., Birmingham, England
Model:	No. 2 Golok
Length overall:	18in.
Blade length:	13in.
Blade shape:	Bellied machete type with drop point
Blade material:	5/32in. thick carbon steel
Edge:	Bevel-ground
Grip:	Wooden handle
Construction:	One-piece slotted wooden handle riveted to three-quarter length tang, with lanyard hole
Sheath:	Composite belt sheath

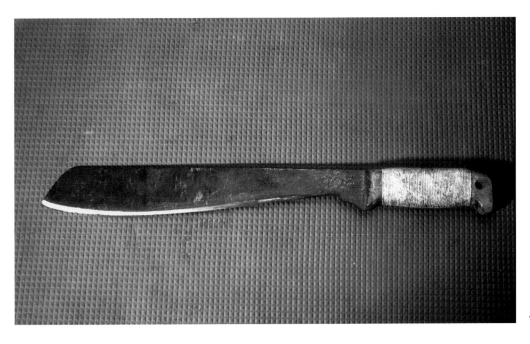

The Hook was conceived as a knife with one purpose: rescue. It is designed to be used to free accident victims quickly and with little chance of causing further injury, as would be all too possible with a normal, straight-bladed knife.

The blade can be hooked round a rope, seat belt or clothing and yanked through, the razor-sharp edge slicing through the toughest materials with relative ease. Speed is of the essence in rescue work, and operators have little time to worry about the blade's follow-through as they slash through obstructions. The advantage of the Hook is that it is virtually impossible to cause an injury with it - the rounded tip will not penetrate flesh and the edge itself is protected.

The Hook is deliberately simple in construction, to keep costs down. It is basically a single piece of 5mm high tensile surgical steel, with contoured grips of beech wood screwed on either side of the tang. The tang extends to form a heavy duty screwdriver/pry bar, which also serves as a windscreen breaker if required, and there is a hole for attaching a lanyard so the Hook can not get lost in the heat of a rescue operation.

The manufacturers claim that the Hook has proved popular with the emergency services in Britain as well as with the prison service, where it is used to cut down prisoners who attempt to commit suicide by hanging.

Manufacturer:	Portfolio Section V Ltd, Stockport, Cheshire, UK
Model:	The Hook
Length overall:	7 7/8in.
Blade length:	2 3/4in.
Blade shape:	Hooked blade with edge on inside, blunt safety tip
Blade material:	5mm thick high tensile surgical steel
Edge:	Hollow-ground
Grip:	Contoured beech wood scales
Construction:	Scales pinned to full-size tang with threaded screws
Features:	Heavy duty screwdriver/windscreen breaker pommel with lanyard hole
Sheath:	Leather or nylon belt pouch

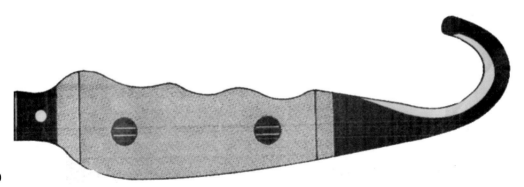

Although designed and marketed as a general purpose knife, Lansky's 'The Knife' has - perhaps unfairly - acquired a reputation as a clandestine fighting weapon because of its all-plastic construction, which makes it difficult to find with conventional detection methods such as X-ray and magnetometer search.

The Knife is moulded in one piece from black ABS plastic. It measures 7in. overall, with a double-edged 3 1/2in. spear point blade. One side has a plain bevel edge, the other is serrated. The grip is chequered, with a finger groove and thumb rest for added grip.

Although its materials and light weight do not particularly lend The Knife to either general field chores or fighting, because of the ease with which it can be hidden it may be used as a clandestine or escape and evasion weapon in situations where the alternative might be no knife at all.

Manufacturer:	Lansky Sharpeners, Buffalo, New York, USA
Model:	LS-17 The Knife
Length overall:	7in.
Blade length:	3 1/2in.
Blade shape:	Spear point
Blade material:	ABS plastic
Edge:	Double-edge bevel-grind, with serrated section on one edge
Grip:	Chequered black plastic with finger groove and thumb rest
Construction:	One-piece moulded plastic
Features:	Lanyard hole. Sheath available

This tool was developed by John 'Lofty' Wiseman, a former survival instructor with the British Special Air Service Regiment and author of several books on survival, in conjunction with designer Ivan Williams. The design shows influence from a variety of edged tools around the world (including the kukri, Machax and Golok), and draws on Wiseman's considerable experience of the tasks that are most important in a survival situation.

'What you need in the wilderness is a knife you can rely on, that does a variety of jobs, and is safe to use', explains Wiseman in an advertisement for his knife. He designed it to tackle a wide range of tasks, ranging from heavy work such as cutting down trees, to preparing game and feathering fire sticks.

The blade is heavy, with the weight forward, which makes it excellent for chopping. The spear point is strong enough for digging and prying, and the back edge is steeply ground for chopping and splitting. At the widest part, the edge is convex, which is good for slashing as well as chopping. Near the handle, the blade narrows and provides a fine edge that can be kept razor sharp for jobs such as feathering sticks for fire-starting.

The handle is moulded Zytel, on a full tang. This sits comfortably in the hand, and is angled downwards to provide a good angle for chopping. There is also a lanyard hole moulded into the grip.

Finally, the sheath has been designed as part of the system. Made of black leather, it has a hanging belt loop and a leg tie. It encases the knife securely, and has a double poppered strap which holds the knife in place until required.

Wiseman's experience really is apparent in the design of this knife and sheath, and anyone who has been in a real life survival situation will appreciate the care and thought that have gone into its design and manufacture.

Manufacturer:	Oakwood Sports, UK
Model:	Lofty Wiseman Survival Tool
Length overall:	15 1/2in.
Blade length:	11in.
Blade shape:	Spear point, upswept machete type
Blade material:	Steel
Edge:	Bevel-ground
Grip:	Moulded Zytel, stainless steel bolster
Construction:	Handle moulded to full length tang
Sheath:	Black leather sheath with belt drop loop and leg tie

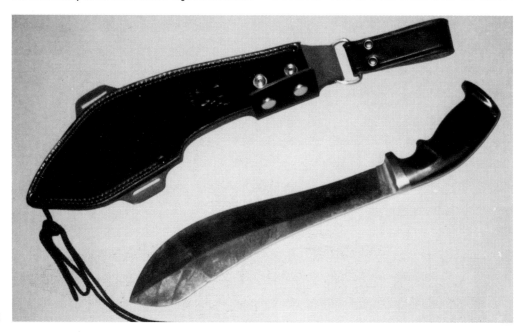

A vital military tool for jungle operations, a machete is used for a wide range of jobs including clearing vegetation for paths and landing sites, constructing shelters, gathering and preparing food. In extremis it may be used as a close-quarter combat weapon.

Ontario's model ON-18 Military Jungle Machete is a typical example, with an 18in. carbon steel blade with a black composition handle fixed to the full tang with three large copper rivets. The blade has a black finish which protects against the elements, as well as cutting down reflections which could give away a soldier's position.

The blade broadens towards the tip, finishing in an upswept edge which meets the straight spine at the tip. This gives the forward-weighted characteristics which make the machete such an effective hacking and chopping tool. In addition to the plain version, there is a sawback model which is identical in all respects except for a saw edge along the middle section of the spine.

The machete comes with a choice of scabbard - a canvas type in olive drab with a belt loop, or a rigid black plastic one with steel clips to fit a military duty belt.

Other models supplied by Ontario offer a similar design but with a variety of blade shapes, including a rounded, partly hooked beak shape (ON-CT3), and a round-ended beavertail (ON-CT4) both 17 1/4in. overall.

Manufacturer:	Ontario Knife Co., Franklinville, New York, USA
Model:	ON-18 Military Jungle Machete
Length overall:	23in.
Blade length:	18in.
Blade shape:	Convex edge with straight spine
Blade material:	Carbon steel with black finish
Edge:	Bevel-ground (sawback version also available)
Grip:	Black composition, with lanyard hole
Construction:	Scales riveted to full-size tang
Sheath:	Choice of OD canvas belt sheath or black plastic sheath with webbing clip and built-in sharpener

This is a relatively new addition to the Ontario product line, and includes several models with different blade sizes and shapes, based firmly on the conventional machete styles. The main difference between these and the regular machete designs is the full knuckle guard which forms a loop from butt to hilt, and gives these machetes a distinctly cutlass-like appearance. The ON-1495 has a clip point Bowie-style blade, which reinforces this impression. The clip point serves the useful purpose of providing a sharp point, while not reducing the machete's effectiveness for chopping, etc.

Manufacturer:	Ontario Knife Co., Franklinville, New York, USA
Model:	ON-1495 Blackie Collins Machete
Length overall:	18in.
Blade length:	12in.
Blade shape:	Clip point Bowie-style machete
Blade material:	Carbon steel with black finish
Edge:	Bevel-ground with false clip edge
Grip:	Black composition, with full knuckle guard
Construction:	Handle riveted to full-size tang
Sheath:	Heavy duty black nylon belt sheath

This is a design that may be seen in bush and jungle areas all over the world, where it is used as an everyday field and agricultural tool. In the hands of paramilitaries and guerrilla forces it becomes a brutal, close-quarters weapon wielded in the same way as a sword, and has been used, for instance, in tribal massacres and repression in central and southern Africa.

The examples shown here are manufactured by Tramontina in Brazil. They are simply made, with hardwood or rubber handle scales riveted to a carbon steel blade. The blade steel is deliberately quite soft, which minimises any tendency for the blade to chip or shatter when used for chopping and hammering, and also makes it easy to sharpen.

The name 'Panga' is sometimes applied to a shorter machete with an upswept blade, such as the 16in. model made by Ralph Martindale & Co. of Sheffield, England.

Manufacturer:	Tramontina, Brazil
Model:	TT-524 Machete
Length overall:	28in. (19in. and 23in. models also available)
Blade length:	22in. (14in., 17in. and 18in. in other models)
Blade shape:	Upswept, convex edge
Blade material:	Carbon steel
Edge:	Bevel-ground
Grip:	Wooden or black rubber
Construction:	Scales riveted to full-size tang
Sheath:	Supplied with or without sheath

This British Royal Navy issue diver's knife was designed by the RN diving school, and is made in Sheffield to Ministry of Defence specifications. It measures 12 4/5in. overall, with a 7 11/16in. double-edged blade made of corrosion-resistant stainless steel. One side of the blade has a plain bevel-ground edge, while the other has deep serrations for cutting rope, webbing, etc. The blade ends in a strong spear point which can be used for prying.

The handle is made of black rubber, and features lateral ridges for extra grip. It has a lanyard hole, and there is a flat stainless steel pommel which can be used for hammering.

The knife comes with a black rubber sheath with leg straps, for wearing on the thigh.

A vital survival and rescue tool for divers, this knife also serves as a lethally effective combat weapon when required.

Manufacturer:	UK Ministry of Defence contractors, Sheffield, England
Model:	RN3
Length overall:	12 4/5in.
Blade length:	7 11/16in.
Blade shape:	Parallel-edge spear point, with serrated back edge
Blade material:	Stainless steel
Edge:	Bevel-ground
Grip:	Black rubber with three lateral ridges, lanyard hole
Construction:	Full-length tang, grip secured with stainless steel pommel
Sheath:	Black rubber sheath with leg straps

line. An ice-pick attachment can be fitted to the butt, where it is retained in place by the pommel.

Users report that this machete performs extremely well at all chopping, slashing and digging tasks, and has proved to be an invaluable camp and field tool. It would also be an effective combat weapon if so required.

Manufacturer:	Saratov Military Factory, Russia
Model:	*Spetsnaz* Machete
Length overall:	15in.
Blade length:	10in.
Blade shape:	Broad square-ended bolo machete style with sawback
Blade material:	High carbon steel
Edge:	Bevel ground
Grip:	Grooved moulded polymer grip, with hollow cavity for survival items; lanyard hole
Construction:	Short tang to allow for hollow handle
Features:	Screw-on pommel cap allows access to handle cavity containing matches, hooks and line; ice-pick attachment

Said to be a standard issue item of the former Soviet Union's elite *Spetsnaz* units, this multi-purpose camp and field tool will chop, dig, cut, pry and much more besides.

The machete weighs 1 1/2 lb and measures 15in. long with a 10in. blade. It has a broad, square-ended machete blade weighted towards the tip. There is a sawback, and a serrated section on the reverse curve cutting edge. A plain edge on the broadest part is suitable for chopping wood, etc., and the square end is also sharpened for digging, etc. The blade features degree markings and a measuring rule.

The blade material is high carbon steel, which the marketing literature rather optimistically claims will never need sharpening. This steel is hard, but any edge will lose its sharpness with use, never mind abuse. However, the machete's edge can quickly be restored with a good sharpening stone.

The handle is made of orange-brown-coloured polymer, and has a hollow section capped with a screw-on pommel. The compartment contains a small collection of survival items, including matches, fishing hooks and

The Spec Plus SP7 is a specialist diver's knife, designed to fulfil a wide range of uses required by military and civilian divers. The blade is double-sided with serrations on both sides for 1 3/4in. near the hilt. These serrations give extra cutting power for rope, webbing, weed and the like. The tip is cut off square, with a false edge which is suitable for prying. The flat-ended pommel allows one to pound the tip into a crevice with the flat of the hand or a rock, using the knife like a chisel.

Materials are chosen to be resistant to salt water and corrosion: the blade is 440A stainless steel, and the handle is black Kraton. The knife comes with a rigid, moulded, black plastic belt sheath, with a stainless steel clip to attach to a military duty belt.

Manufacturer:	Ontario Knife Co., Franklinville, New York, USA
Model:	SP7 Diver Probe
Length overall:	11in.
Blade length:	5 3/4in.
Blade shape:	Spear truncated with chisel point
Blade material:	0.187in. thick 440A stainless steel, black epoxy powder coated
Edge:	Double. Bevel-ground, with 1 3/4in. serrated section either side
Grip:	Black Kraton grooved handle with flat oversized pommel incorporating lanyard hole
Construction:	Kraton handle moulded on to tang
Sheath:	Rigid plastic sheath with nylon loop and clip for military duty belt

This Spec Plus machete is a versatile tool which deserves to be used more regularly in the field than its 'survival' tag implies. The simple, rectangularly shaped blade measures 10in. long, and is made from a solid bar of 1/4in. thick carbon steel. This is sharpened along one edge and across the end, leaving plenty of meat in the blade for work like prying and digging. The blade retains weight too, giving a powerful chopping action - good for clearing brush, cutting materials for a shelter or raft, and preparing wood for a fire.

On the spine of the blade is an effective saw edge, with the teeth set to cut on the away stroke. The teeth are cut like a proper saw blade, alternately set right and left. This ensures that the saw removes its own thickness of material, so that the blade does not jam as it cuts into wood or bone.

The Kraton rubber handle is shaped to fill the hand well, with guards at front and back for protection. The lateral grooves give added grip, and the soft Kraton rubber cushions the hand against the shock of heavy chopping.

The belt sheath is made from black Cordura nylon, with leather press-studded straps to hold the machete firmly in place until required. A leg tie prevents the sheath from flapping against the leg when the wearer runs.

Manufacturer:	Ontario Knife Co., Franklinville, New York, USA
Model:	SP8 Survival Machete
Length overall:	15 1/8in.
Blade length:	10in.
Blade shape:	Rectangular
Blade material:	1/4in. thick 1095 carbon steel, black epoxy powder coated
Edge:	Double milled, bevel-ground, with saw back
Grip:	Black Kraton grooved handle incorporating lanyard hole
Construction:	Kraton handle moulded on to tang
Sheath:	Black Cordura and leather belt sheath with leg tie

A relatively new addition to the Spec Plus line, the Broad Point Survival has a symmetrical, double-edged spear point blade which is shaped like a smaller version of the Combat Smatchet. This gives good chopping and slicing characteristics for what is a relatively short blade, and may also be used for prying and digging. Although not its primary purpose, this blade would also be effective as a close-quarters combat weapon.

The handle is made of black Kraton rubber, with lateral grooves for extra grip. The pommel is flat-ended, and is screwed on to the threaded end of the full-length tang. It may be used as a hammer, or pounded with a rock, log or the flat of the hand to drive the spear point of the blade into an object. The shape of the spear point provides the strength necessary to stand up to this kind of use.

Manufacturer:	Ontario Knife Co., Franklinville, New York, USA
Model:	SP9 Broad Point Survival
Length overall:	11 3/8in.
Blade length:	6in.
Blade shape:	Leaf-shaped spear point
Blade material:	1095 carbon steel, black epoxy powder coated
Edge:	Bevel-ground
Grip:	Black Kraton grooved handle with flat-ended pommel incorporating lanyard hole
Construction:	Milled butt cap screwed on to threaded tang
Sheath:	Black Cordura and leather belt sheath with lanyard

The Spec Plus Marine Raider takes the old 'iron mistress' Bowie style and applies modern materials and manufacturing techniques to produce a distinctive looking knife with a multitude of uses.

The deep, 9 5/8in. clip point blade is heavy enough for chopping, but still effective for more delicate slicing and cutting. The clip point provides a sharp point which may be used for surprisingly delicate jobs. A good all-round camp and field tool, this knife is also a fearsome combat weapon with a shape that is as intimidating as it is effective.

Where the traditional Bowie would have a plain blade and natural wood or bone handle, this modern version has a protective black epoxy powder coating on the blade and a moulded Kraton rubber handle. These modern materials provide better performance in adverse conditions, with extra resistance to the elements.

Manufacturer:	Ontario Knife Co., Franklinville, New York, USA
Model:	SP10 Marine Raider
Length overall:	15in.
Blade length:	9 5/8in.
Blade shape:	Deep 'iron mistress' style Bowie
Blade material:	1095 carbon steel, black epoxy powder coated
Edge:	Bevel-ground
Grip:	Black Kraton grooved handle incorporating lanyard hole
Construction:	Kraton handle moulded on to tang
Sheath:	Black Cordura and leather belt sheath with lanyard

The large, forward-weighted, downward-curved blade of the Spec Plus Bolo owes a great deal to the Gurkha kukri, but is combined with a straight grip of black Kraton rubber in the familiar Spec Plus style. The end result is a hefty knife with immense cutting and chopping power - equally effective for camp and field tasks or for combat.

Like the kukri, the Bolo's blade broadens out towards the last third of its 10in. length. This places the bulk of its weight well forward for a powerful chopping stroke. It also provides a reverse curve cutting edge nearer the grip. The reverse curve is acknowledged as one of the most effective edge shapes for cutting and slashing - like a scythe, it keeps the edge pressed tightly against the work as the blade is drawn through. The drop point is less sharply angled than a clip point style but still gives effective penetration for stabbing.

Like other heavy knives in the Spec Plus range, the well shaped rubber Kraton handle provides excellent grip and cushions the hand against the shock of chopping.

Manufacturer:	Ontario Knife Co., Franklinville, New York, USA
Model:	SP11 Bolo
Length overall:	15 1/8in.
Blade length:	10in.
Blade shape:	Drop point bolo style
Blade material:	1095 carbon steel, black epoxy powder coated
Edge:	Flat-ground
Grip:	Black Kraton grooved handle incorporating lanyard hole
Construction:	Kraton handle moulded on to tang
Sheath:	Black Cordura and leather belt sheath with lanyard

The United Cutlery Special Ops Jungle Machete is said to have been designed specifically for the US Navy SEALs by custom knifemaker George Lainhart. Smaller and more compact than a regular machete, it aims to retain all the weight and chopping power of a full-sized machete.

This machete has a deep, straight backed blade of 3/16in. thick ATS34 stainless steel, hardened to 56-57 on the Rockwell scale. ATS34 is renowned for its strength and edge holding. The blade is coated with a high tech black polymer called 'Roguard' to protect the steel and reduce reflections.

The handle is moulded from black Kraton rubber, with chequered panels for extra grip. It has a bellied shape, and large guards at hilt and butt to protect the hand. The lanyard hole is formed from a stainless steel tube which also serves to pin the handle to the full-length tang.

This is a hefty chopping tool which would be highly effective both for camp and field chores and for combat. Its modern materials offer excellent resistance to adverse conditions and should continue to provide superior performance for many years.

The sheath is made from black Latigo leather which is treated with a fungicide to resist mildew in jungle conditions. It has several attachment options, so that it may be worn on a belt, attached to webbing with Alice clips, or tied to load-carrying equipment using the four grommet holes.

Manufacturer:	United Cutlery, Sevierville, Tennessee, USA
Model:	UC934 Special Ops Jungle Machete
Length overall:	14 11/16in.
Blade length:	9 3/8in.
Blade shape:	Straight back convex edge machete
Blade material:	3/16in. thick ATS34 stainless steel, 56-57 Rc, black 'Roguard' polymer coated
Edge:	Bevel-ground
Grip:	Chequered black Kraton handle with lanyard hole
Construction:	Kraton handle moulded on to full-length tang and secured with tubular stainless steel pin which also forms lanyard hole
Sheath:	Black Latigo leather treated with fungicide; includes belt strap, grommets and Alice clip slots